Alphonse Daudet

Tartarin on the Alps

Illustrated by Aranda, de Beaumont, Montenard, Myrbach, and Rossi. Engraved by Guillaume brothers, tr. by Henry Frith

Alphonse Daudet

Tartarin on the Alps

Illustrated by Aranda, de Beaumont, Montenard, Myrbach, and Rossi. Engraved by Guillaume brothers, tr. by Henry Frith

ISBN/EAN: 9783337092375

Printed in Europe, USA, Canada, Australia, Japan

Cover: Foto ©ninafisch / pixelio.de

More available books at **www.hansebooks.com**

ALPHONSE DAUDET

Tartarin on the Alps

Illustrated

BY ARANDA, DE BEAUMONT, MONTENARD, MYRBACH.
AND ROSSI.

Engraved by GUILLAUME Brothers

TRANSLATED BY HENRY FRITH

LONDON
GEORGE ROUTLEDGE AND SONS
BROADWAY, LUDGATE HILL
GLASGOW AND NEW YORK

1888

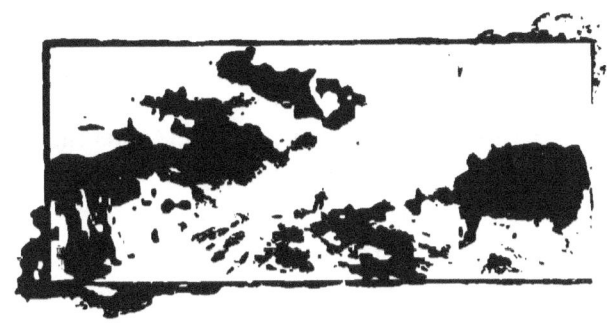

I

𝔞 *An apparition on the Rigi-Kulm.—Who is he?—What was said at the table d'hôte.—Rice and Prunes.—An improvised ball.—The Unknown signs his name in the hotel register.—P. C. A.*

On the 10th of August, 1880, at the fabled hour of sunset, so much belauded by Joanne's and Bædeker's Guide-Books, a thick, yellow fog, rendered more puzzling by a whirling snow-storm, enveloped the summit of the Rigi (*Regina montium*) and that immense hotel—which presents such an extraordinary appearance in the barren landscape of hills the Rigi-Kulm, glazed like an observatory, massive as a citadel, wherein for a day and a night a crowd of sun-worshipping tourists is located.

While awaiting the second dinner-gong, the occupants of this extensive and sumptuous caravanserai, chilled in their bed-rooms, or seated listlessly on the divans in the reading-room, in the damp semi-warmth of the lighted stoves, were gazing—in default of the promised splendours—at the whirling snowflakes in the air, or at the lighting of the great lamps before the entrance, whose double glasses quivered in the tempestuous wind.

Fancy having ascended so high and having come from all parts of the world for this! O Bædeker!

Suddenly something emerged from the fog and advanced towards the hotel, with the clanking of iron, an exaggeration of its movements being caused by the unusual surroundings.

At twenty paces distant through the snow, the idle tourists, with their noses flattened against the windows, the little girls, whose hair was cut short like boys', took this apparition for a straying cow, then for a *rétameur* carrying his tools.

At ten paces the apparition again changed its appearance, and showed a cross-bow on its shoulder, and the casque of an archer of the middle ages on its head, an object still less likely to be met with on the mountains than a cow or a pedlar.

When he reached the steps, the archer was only a fat man, thickset, and broad-shouldered, who stopped to puff and blow, and to shake the snow from his gaiters, which were of yellow cloth like his cap, and from his knitted comforter, which permitted scarcely anything to be seen of his face but two enormous tufts of grey whisker and a pair of green spectacles like the eye-pieces of a stereoscope. An ice-axe, an alpenstock, a knapsack, a coil of rope, *crampons*, and iron hooks suspended from the belt of a Norfolk jacket with deep flaps, completed the accoutrement of this perfect Alpine climber.

Upon the desolate summit of Mont Blanc or the Finsteraarhorn, such a "get up" would have been suitable enough; but at the Rigi-Kulm, a few paces from the railway!

The Alpinist, it is true, came from the side opposite to the station, and the condition of his leggings bore witness to the long tramp he had had through the snow and mire.

For a moment he gazed at the hotel and its dependencies, surprised to find, at six thousand feet above the level of the sea, a building of such a size, with its glazed galleries, its colonnades, its seven ranges of windows, and the wide flight of steps between two rows of lamps which gave to the top of the mountain something of the appearance of the Place de l'Opéra in a wintry twilight.

But however greatly surprised he may have been the occupants of the hotel seemed much more so; and when he entered the wide vestibule, a curious, pushing crowd filled the doorways of the *salles;* gentlemen grasping billiard cues, or with newspapers in their hands; ladies holding their books or work; while at the end, up the staircase, heads were protruded over the banisters and between the chains of the "lift."

The new-comer spoke in a loud voice, a strong basso-profundo, a *creux du Midi*, which sounded like a pair of cymbals:

"*Coquin de sort!* Here's weather——"

Suddenly he stopped, took off his cap and spectacles.

He was choking.

The glare of the lights, the heat of the gas and of the stoves, contrasting with the black cold night outside, the sumptuous appearance of the hotel, the lofty vestibule, the richly-laced porters with "REGINA MONTIUM" in gold letters on their caps, the white ties of the *maitres d'hôtel*, and the battalion of Swiss female servants in their national costumes, who came running up at the sound of the gong—all this impressed him for a second, not for more than one.

He felt himself the cynosure of all eyes, and immediately recovered his self-possession, like a comedian before a full house.

"*Monsieur desire* ——?"

It was the manager who asked him the question, softly; a very well got up manager, with a striped jacket, carefully tended whiskers, and *très chic*, in fact.

The mountaineer, without any emotion, demanded a room, "a nice little room at any rate," quite as much at his ease with this majestic manager as with an old school-friend.

He was very nearly putting himself out, though, when the Bernese servant approached him, candle in hand, resplendent in her gold lace and tulle-decked sleeves, to inquire whether Monsieur would like to go up in the lift. If she had suggested the commission of a crime our hero could not have been more indignant.

A lift! for him! for *him!* His exclamation and his gesture caused his paraphernalia to rattle again.

As suddenly appeased he said to the Swiss maid in a pleasant tone: "*Pedibus cum jambis, ma belle chatte,*" and he mounted behind her, his wide back occupying the width of the stairs, knocking against people on the way up, while the whole hotel rang with the question, "Who is he?" expressed in every language under the sun. Then the second dinner-bell sounded, and no one troubled himself or herself any more concerning this extraordinary individual.

A sight indeed is the *salle-à-manger* of the Rigi-Kulm.

Six hundred guests seated around an immense horse-shoe table on which dishes of rice and prunes alternate in long files with green plants, reflecting in their clear or brown sauce the lights of the lustres or the gilding of the panelled ceiling.

As at all Swiss *tables d'hôte*, this rice and these prunes divide the diners into two rival factions, and the looks of hatred or covetousness bestowed upon the dessert dishes is quite sufficient to enable the spectator to divine to which party the guests belong. The Rice

Party betray themselves by their pallor, the Prunes by their congested appearance.

On this particular evening the latter were in the majority, and included all the most important personages, quite European celebrities, such as the great historian Astier-Réhu of the French Academy; the Baron de Stolz, an old Austro-Hungarian diplomatist; Lord Chippendale, a member of the Jockey Club with his niece (?) (hum !); the illustrious Professor Schwanthaler, of Bonn University; a Peruvian general and his eight daughters.

To all these the Rice faction could only oppose as *vedettes* a Belgian Senator and his family; Madame Schwanthaler, the wife of the Professor aforesaid; and an Italian tenor on his way from Russia, exhibiting upon the table-cloth a pair of sleeve-links as large as saucers.

These double and opposing currents no doubt gave an air of lassitude and stiffness to the *table d'hôte*. How otherwise can we account for the silence of these six hundred persons, stiff, surly, defiant, with that supreme contempt which they affected to possess one for the other? A superficial observer would have attributed it to the stupid Anglo-Saxon reserve which now gives the tone to the travelling world.

But no! Human beings do not thus hate each other at

first sight; turning up their noses at each other; sneering, and glancing superciliously at one another in the absence of introductions. There must have been something else!

Rice and Prunes, I tell you. There you have the explanation of the mournful silence that weighed down upon the dinner at the Rigi-Kulm, which, considering the number and the varied nationalities of the guests, ought to have been very animated and noisy; something like what one would imagine a meal at the foot of the Tower of Babel might have been.

The mountaineer entered the room—a little perplexed in this assembly of Trappists beneath the glare of the lustres—coughed loudly without any one taking any notice of him, and seated himself in his place next the last comer, at the end of the table. Unaccoutred now, he was simply an ordinary tourist, but of a very amiable appearance; bald, rotund, his beard thick and pointed, a fine nose, thick and somewhat fierce eyebrows, with a pleasant manner and appearance.

Rice or Prune! No one knew yet.

Scarcely had he seated himself, when, quitting his place with a bound, he exclaimed, "*Outre!* a draught!" and rushed to an empty chair turned down at the centre of the table.

He was stopped by one of the Swiss female attendants, a native of the canton of Uri, wearing little silver chains and white stomacher.

"Monsieur, that is engaged."

Then, from the table, a young lady, of whom he could see nothing but a mass of fair hair relieved by a neck white as virgin snow, said, without turning round, and with a foreign accent:

"This seat is at liberty; my brother is not well, and will not come down to dinner."

"Ill?" asked the mountaineer, with an interested, almost affectionate, manner, as he seated himself. "Ill? Not dangerously, *au moins?*"

He pronounced the last words *au mouain*, and they reasserted themselves with some other vocal parasites "*hé, qué, té, zou, vé, vaï, allons,*" &c., that still further accentuated his southern tongue, which was no doubt displeasing to the youthful blonde; for she only replied to him with a stony stare—from eyes of deep, dark blue.

The neighbour on his right was not encouraging either. He was the Italian tenor, with a low forehead, very moist eyes, and Hectoring moustaches which he twirled in

an irritable manner, for had he not been separated from his pretty neighbour? But the good mountaineer had a habit of talking while he was eating—he thought it good for his digestion.

" *Vé!* What pretty buttons," he remarked aloud to himself, as he glanced at the Italian's sleeve-studs. "Those notes of music, inlaid with the jasper, have a charming effect" "*un effet charmain*"!

His strident tones rang through the silent *salle*, without producing the least echo.

"Surely monsieur is a singer, *qué?*"

"*Non capisco*," growled the Italian through his moustache.

For a moment the man devoted himself to

his dinner without speaking but the food choked him. At length, as his opposite neighbour, the Austro-Hungarian diplomatist, attempted to reach the mustard-pot with his small, aged, shaking hands, enveloped in mittens, our hero passed it politely to him, saying, "*A votre service, monsieur le baron*," for he had heard him thus addressed.

Unfortunately poor M. de Stoltz, notwithstanding the cunning and ingenious air which he had contracted in the pursuit of Chinese diplomacy, had long ago lost his speech and his ideas, and was travelling around the mountains with the view of finding them again. He opened his eyes wide and gazed at the unknown face, and then shut them again without saying anything. It would have taken ten old diplomats of his intellectual power to find the formula of acknowledgment.

At this new failure the mountaineer made a grimace, and the rough manner in which he seized the bottle gave one the idea that he was going to break, with it, the cracked head of the old diplomatist. But no such thing. It was merely to offer his neighbour a glass of wine, but she did not hear him, being lost in a murmured conversation—a chirping, sweet and lively, in an unknown tongue—with two young people close by. She leaned forward, she became animated. He could see her little curls shimmer in the light against a tiny ear, transparent and rosy-tinted. Polish?

Russian? Norwegian? Well, certainly Northern; and a pretty little song of his native district escaped the lips of the Southerner, who quietly began to hum:

> "*O coumtesso gènto,*
> *Estelo dou Nord*
> *Qué la neu argento,*
> *Qu'Amour friso en or.*"

Everybody at table turned round: they all thought he had gone mad. He blushed and kept himself quiet in his place, not moving except to push violently away the dish of sacred fruit which they passed to him.

"Prunes! Never in my life!"

This was too much.

There was a great movement of chairs. The Academician, Lord Chippendale, the Professor of Bonn, and some other notables of the party, rose and quitted the room by way of protest.

The Rice Party almost immediately followed them when they perceived the stranger push away from him the other dessert dish as violently as the former.

Neither Rice nor Prune! What then?

All the guests retired, and the silence was truly glacial as the people, with bowed heads and with the corners of their mouths disdain-

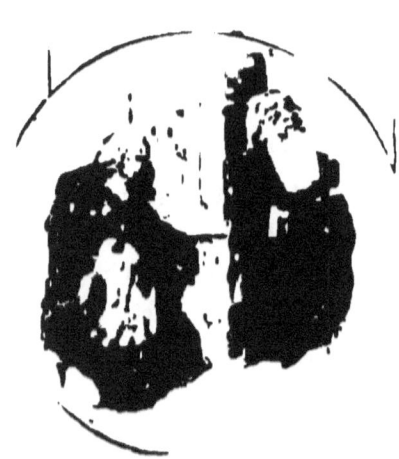

fully drawn down, passed in front of the unhappy individual who remained alone in the immense dining-room, inclined *de faire une trempette* after the manner of his country, but kept down by the universal disdain!

My friends, never despise any one. Contempt is the resource of upstarts, of *parvenus*, of ugly people, of fools,— the mask beneath which they hide their insignificance, sometimes their poverty, and which dispense with mind, with judgment, with g odness. All hump-backed people are contemptuous; all the wry-nosed ones scowl and display disdain when they meet with a straight nose!

Our good mountaineer knew that. Having

passed his fortieth year some time before
—that "*palier du quatrième*" where man
finds and picks up the magic key which opens
life to him to the very end, showing him the

monotonous and deceptive perspective of
years, becoming cognisant, besides, of his
worth, the importance of his mission, and of
the great name that he bears—the opinion of
such people scarcely affected him. Besides
he had only to mention his name—to cry out,
"It is I"—to change into profound respect
all these haughty lips. But the *incognito*
amused him.

He only suffered because he could not talk and make a noise, give vent to his opinions, shake hands, tap people familiarly on the shoulder, and call them by their Christian names. That is what oppressed him at the Rigi-Kulm.

But above all was the fact that he had no one to talk to!

"It will give me the pip, I am quite sure of that," he said to himself, as he wandered about the hotel, not knowing what to do with himself.

He entered the *café*, as empty as a church on a week-day, called the waiter "my good friend," ordered a "mocha without sugar—*qué*." As the waiter did not ask "Why without sugar?" the Alpinist added quickly, "That is a habit I contracted in Algeria when I was hunting there."

He was going to tell him about it, but the man had fled away like a phantom to Lord Chippendale, who was stretched upon a couch and demanding in a melancholy voice, "Tchimppègne, Tchimppègne." The cork popped cheerfully, and then nothing more was heard but the roaring of the wind in the massive chimney and the chilling click of the snow against the window-panes.

Very doleful also was the reading-room; all the papers engaged. Those hundreds of heads bent around the long green tables under the reflectors. From time to time was heard a sneeze or a cough, or the rustling of a page turned by a reader. Standing upright and motionless, looking down upon the calm of the reading-room, with their backs to the stove, were the two pontiffs of official history, Schwanthaler and Astier-Réhu — equally solemn and equally dry—whom a curious fatality had brought together at the top of the Rigi after a lapse of thirty years, during which period they had been vilifying each other, and pulling each other to pieces in abusive notes, as Schwanthaler the blockhead, and Astier-Réhu *vir ineptissimus*.

You may imagine the reception the benevolent Alpinist had when he took a seat at the corner of the fire-place, to hear a few instructive words. From the height of the two Caryatids fell suddenly upon him one of those cold currents which he so greatly dreaded: he rose, paced the room, as much for appearance sake as to warm himself; then he opened the bookcase. Some English

novels were in it, mixed up with heavy Bibles and some well-thumbed volumes of the Swiss Alpine Club: he took one of these, with the intention of reading it in bed, but he was stopped at the door, as the regulations of the hotel do not permit any one to carry books up stairs to the bedrooms.

Then, continuing to wander about, he opened the door of the billiard-room, where the Italian tenor was playing by himself, bending himself into graceful attitudes, and displaying his wristbands for the edification

of his pretty neighbour, who was seated on a divan between two young men, to whom she was reading a letter. As the mountaineer entered she paused, and one of the young fellows got up   he was the taller, a sort of *moujik*, *homme chien*, with hairy hands, and black locks, flat and shiny, joined to an untrimmed beard. He made two paces towards the newcomer, and looked at him so provokingly and so ferociously that the kindly Alpinist, without demanding any explanation, executed a half-turn to the right prudently and with dignity.

"They are not very pleasant people in the North," he said aloud, as he slammed the door behind him loudly to let the savage perceive that he was not afraid of him.

The *salon* was now his only remaining refuge. He entered it. *Coquin de sort!* The Morgue, good people, the Morgue of Mont St. Bernard—wherein the monks exhibit the unfortunate travellers who have been found in the snow in the various attitudes in which they were frozen to death—that was what the *salon* of the Rigi-Kulm was!

All the ladies, in frozen silence, in groups upon the circular seats, or had fallen even on isolated chairs, here and there. All the young ladies, immovable, under the lamps on the round tables, still holding in their hands the album, the magazine, or the embroidery which they were holding when the cold seized them; and amongst them were the daughters of the general, the eight little Peruvians with their saffron complexions, their tresses in disorder, the bright-coloured ribbons of their dresses contrasting with the more subdued tones of the English fashions, poor little *pays-chauds* whom one can imagine grinning and grimacing at the tops of the cocoa-nut trees, and whom, more than the other victims, it pained one to see in that state of silence and congelation. Then at the end of the room, at the piano, was the death's-head profile of the old diplomatist, his little mitten-covered hands lay motionless upon the key-board, his face reflecting the yellow tinge of the keys.

Betrayed by his strength and his memory, lost in a polka of his own composition, which he always recommenced at the same movement in default of recollecting the *coda*, the unhappy de Stoltz had gone to sleep while playing it, and with him all the elderly ladies of the Rigi, nodding, in their sleep, their curls, or those lace caps like the crust of a *vol-au-*

vent of which Englishwomen are so fond, and which is part of the *cant voyageur*.

The entrance of the Alpinist did not wake them, and he himself was creeping into a seat, overcome by the glacial atmosphere, when some loud and cheering sounds proceeded from the vestibule, where three musicians (a harp, violin, and flute—those wandering minstrels of such piteous mien, with long coats down to their heels, who frequent Swiss hotels) were tuning their instruments. At the very first notes our hero jumped up as if galvanised.

"*Zou!* bravo! Go ahead with the music!"

There he was in an instant, opening the doors, treating the musicians liberally to champagne, feeling somewhat intoxicated himself, though he drank nothing, with this music, which gave him life. He imitated the cornet, he imitated the harp, snapped his fingers together above his head, rolled his eyes, cut a few capers, to the profound astonishment of the tourists who had rushed from all sides at the uproar. Then, roughly, at the first notes of one of Strauss's waltzes, which the musicians attacked with the fury of

veritable Tzigans, the Alpinist, perceiving at
the door of the *salon* the wife of Professor
Schwanthaler, a little chubby Viennese lady,
sprightly in appearance and still young— notwithstanding her hair was sprinkled with grey

— rushed at her, seized her round the waist,
and dragged her out, calling at the same time
to the others, " Come, then ! waltz away ! "

The impetus was given ; the entire hotel,
thawed and tumultuous now, was carried away
by it. They danced in the vestibule, in the
salon, around the long green table in the
reading-room. And it was this devil of a
fellow who had set them all going ! Never-

theless he danced no more; he was out of breath after a few turns; but he superintended the ball, pressed the musicians, made up the couples for the dances, threw the Professor of Bonn into the arms of an old Englishwoman, and the most frisky of the Peruvian young ladies upon the austere Astier-Réhu.

Resistance was impossible. This terrible Alpinist carried you away in a perfect whirlwind! "*Et zou! et zou!*" No more disdain, no more hatred. There were now neither Rices nor Prunes! All were waltzers. The madness quickly spread and reached every story; and in the enormous bay of the staircase might have been seen, up to the sixth *étage*, turning around the pilasters with the rigidity of the automata outside a musical *chalet*, the heavy coloured gowns of the Swiss female servants!

Ah, the wind may blow now if it please! let it shake the lamps, let it moan and whistle through the telegraph wires, and whirl the snow in spiral storms over the deserted summit of the mountain! Here all is warm and comfortable; and all were settled for the night.

"All the same, I will go to bed myself," thought the worthy mountaineer.

He seizes his key and his chamber candlestick; at the first floor he pauses a moment to enjoy the sight of his work, to watch the crowd of stuck-up people whom he has compelled to amuse and unstiffen themselves.

A Swiss woman, out of breath with her interrupted dance, presented him a pen and the hotel register.

"If I may venture to request monsieur to inscribe his name—?"

He hesitated an instant. Must he do so? Cannot he preserve his *incognito?*

After all, what matter? Suppose that the intelligence of his arrival at the Rigi should reach the valleys, no one will know for what reason he had come to Switzerland. And then what a joke it would be in the morning.

He took the pen, and with a careless hand, beneath the names of Astier-Réhu, Schwanthaler, and all the other illustrious personages, he signed that name which eclipsed them all—his own: then he ascended to his bedroom without even turning round to see the effect which he was confident he had made.

Behind him the Swiss waitress was reading—

TARTARIN DE TARASCON ;

and underneath it—

P. C. A.

She read that, this Bernese young woman and was not overcome. She did not know what P. C. A. signified. She had never heard of " Dardarin."

Savage ! *vai !*

II

Tarascon, five minutes' stoppage.—The Alpine Club.—Explanation of P. C. A.—Rabbits of the warren and of the cabbage-garden.—"This is my will."—The "Sirop de cadavre."—First ascent.—Tartarin mounts his spectacles.

WHEN the name of "Tarascon" vibrates along the Paris, Lyons, and Mediterranean Line, and in the clear blue vault of the Provençal sky, heads of curious people are protruded from the windows of the carriages of the express train, and from compartment to compartment the travellers say to each other—

"Ah, this is Tarascon! let us see something of Tarascon."

What they do see of it is, however, nothing out of the common : a small, quiet, clean town, some turrets, some roofs, a bridge over the Rhone. But the Tarascon sunlight and its wonderful mirage effects, so fruitful in surprises, in inventions, in bewildering *cocasseries;* the cheerful little inhabitants, scarcely bigger than a chick-pea, who reflect and epitomise the instincts of all the French people of the South, are lively, brisk, chatty, imaginative, comic, impressionable,—that is what the passengers by the express get a glimpse of, and that is what makes the place popular.

In certain memorable pages which our modesty prevents us from particularising, the historiographer of Tarascon formerly attempted to depict those pleasant days at the little club, singing its "romances"—every one his own—and in default of game, organising curious shooting-parties *à la casquette*.[1]

---

[1] This is what was said of the local sport in the *Prodigious Adventures of Tartarin of Tarascon:*

Then the war came the "black times," as they call it at Tarascon—its heroic defence, the torpedo-lined esplanade, the club and the Café de la Comédie rendered impregnable; all the inhabitants enrolled as Free Companions—embellished with death's heads and cross-bones, all beards grown, and such a display made of hatchets, cutlasses, and American revolvers that the unfortunate inhabitants were afraid to venture out in the streets for fear of each other.

Many years have passed since the war, many almanacs have been burned, but Tarascon has not been forgotten; and renouncing the futile distractions of a past time, only considers how to turn its blood and muscle to profit in future revenge.

At length the old club itself, abjuring *bouillotte* and *bésigue*, was transformed into the

---

" After a good breakfast in the open country each one of the sportsmen took his cap, threw it with all his strength into the air, and fired at it 'flying' with No. 5, No. 6, or No. 2 shot, according to the regulations. He who hit his cap oftenest was proclaimed King of the Sport, and returned in the evening to Tarascon in triumph—his riddled cap at the end of his gun—amidst the barking of dogs and the flourish of trumpets."

Alpine Club, after the pattern of the famous Alpine Club in London, whose members have sustained its renown even in the Indies.

There is, however, this difference between the clubs - that the Tarasconnais, instead

of expatriating themselves with the view of conquering strange and distant mountains, are content with what they have in their hands, or rather under their feet, at the gates of their town.

The Alps of Tarascon? No, but the *Alpines*, that chain of little hills perfumed with thyme and lavender; neither very difficult nor very

"Planted on the summits of the *Alpines* the flag of the club—the silver-spangled dragon."

high (some 450 to 600 feet in elevation above the level of the sea), which form a horizon of blue waves to the Provençal roads, and which the local imagination has supplied with fabulous and characteristic names, such as *le Mont-Terrible, le Bout-du-Monde, le Pic-des-Géants,* &c.

It is a pleasant sight on a Sunday morning to see the Tarasconnais fully accoutred, with ice-axe, knapsack, and tent on his back, go forth, preceded by clarions, to make the ascent of which the *Forum*—the local journal—gives such a flourishing and descriptive account, with an exaggeration of epithets, "abysses, ravines, terrible gorges," as if it were describing an ascent in the Himalayas. Just think that in this pastime the natives have acquired new strength, the "double muscles" formerly the attributes of the good, brave, heroic Tartarin only.

If Tarascon epitomised the South, Tartarin epitomised Tarascon. He was not only the first citizen of the town, he was its soul, its genius; he knew all about it. He was acquainted with its ancient exploits, its triumphs of song (oh, that duet from *Robert le Diable* at the chemist's!), with the astounding Odyssey of its lion-hunts from which he brought back that splendid camel, the last in Algeria, which has since died full of years and honours, the skeleton of which is in the town museum amongst the Tarasconnais curiosities.

Tartarin himself had not deteriorated; he had still good teeth, a bright eye, notwithstanding his fifty years; and always conserved that extraordinary imagination which brought near and enlarged objects with the power of a telescope. It was of him that the brave commander Bravida said, " *C'est un lapin.*"

Two rabbits, rather. For in Tartarin, as in all the Tarasconnais, there is a warren and a cabbage breed, very clearly marked. The rabbit of the warren is a rover—an adventurous animal; the cabbage-rabbit is domesticated— a stay-at-home, having an extraordinary horror of fatigue, of draughts, and of all the contingencies which may bring death in their train.

We all know that this prudence never prevented him from showing himself brave, and even heroic, on occasion; but it is quite permissible to inquire what business he had on the Rigi (*Regina montium*) at his age, when he had so dearly purchased the right to his ease and comfort.

To such a question the infamous Costecalde only could reply.

Costecalde, a gun maker by trade, represented a type rare in Tarascon. Envy—base, malignant envy—visible in the curl of the thin lips, and in a kind of yellow steam which, rising from the liver in puffs, swelled his large, shaven face into uneven ridges as if produced by the blows of a hammer —like an ancient medal of Tiberius or Caracalla. Envy with him was a disease which he did not even attempt to hide, and with that

fine Tarasconic temperament, which is gushing enough, he used to say when speaking of his infirmity, "You do not know how bad it is"!

Costecalde's tormentor naturally was Tartarin. All that glory for one man! To him ever; always to him! And slowly, surely, like the termite in the gilded wood of the idol, for twenty years he had been sapping and undermining this great reputation, moth-eating it as it were. When in the evening, at the club, Tartarin would relate his combats with the lion, his hunting in the Sahara, Costecalde would indulge in little sniggering laughs, and incredulous shakes of the head.

"But the skins at least, Costecalde, the lion-skins which he sent us, which are yonder in the club-room?"

"*Tè! pardi.* And the furs; do not you

think that there is any want of them in Algeria?"

"But the marks of the bullets, quite round, in the heads?"

"And on the other hand, was it not at the time of our cap-hunting that we used to find, in the hatters' shops, caps with bullet-holes, and riddled with shot, for the unskilful marksmen?"

No doubt the fame of Tartarin, the beast-slayer, remained superior to these attacks; but the Alpinist in his own house listened to all the criticism, and Costecalde did not spare him, furious that they had named as President of the Alpine Club a man who was ageing visibly, and whose habits, contracted in Algeria, disposed him to laziness.

Rarely did Tartarin take part in any of the ascents; he contented himself by accompanying the climbers with his good wishes, and in reading to the full assembly, with much rolling of eyes, and emphasis which made ladies grow pale, the dramatic records of the expeditions.

Costecalde, on the contrary, dry, muscular, nervous, "*Jambe de coq,*" as they called him, always climbed first of all ; he had made all the ascents of the *Alpines* one by one, and had planted upon their lofty summits the flag of the club, the silver-spangled *Tarasque* or dragon. Nevertheless, he was only the Vice-President (V. P. C. A.), but he was working so well that evidently at the next election Tartarin would be ousted.

Advised of this by his associates, our hero was at first terribly disgusted; the evil spirit which ingratitude and injustice will raise in the best minds seized upon him. He had a great mind to give the whole thing up—to emigrate—to cross the bridge, and live in Beaucaire amongst the Volsques. But he grew calmer after a while.

To leave his little house, his garden, his cherished habits, to renounce his chair as President of the Alpine Club he had founded, to give up the majestic P. C. A. which embellished and distinguished his card, his writing paper, even the lining of his hat! It was not to be thought of! It was impossible! *Vé!* Then suddenly there occurred to him a perfectly miraculous notion.

As a matter of fact the exploits of Costecalde were confined to his expeditions in the *Alpines*. Why should not Tartarin, during the three months which must intervene between that time and the election,

attempt some grand adventure? why should not he plant upon the highest summits in Europe (the Jungfrau and Mont Blanc for instance) the banner of his club?

What a triumph would await him on his

return, what a slap in the face it would be for Costecalde when the *Forum* would have published the narrative of the ascent ! How after that could he dare to dispute the possession of the chairmanship?

With all speed he went to work: he had sent to him secretly from Paris a number of special works, such as Whymper's *Scrambles in the Alps*, Tyndall's *Among the Glaciers*, Stephen d'Arve's *Mont Blanc*, the *Alpine Journals* (both Swiss and English); and he fuddled his brain with a string of Alpine terms,—chimneys, *couloirs, moulins, névé, séracs, moraines, rotures*,—without knowing precisely what they all meant.

At night his dreams were disturbed by interminable *glissades*, and sheer falls into bottomless crevasses! Avalanches overwhelmed him; *arêtes* of ice impaled his body on the way; and long after he was awake and had consumed his morning chocolate, which he always took in bed, he retained the agony and the oppression of the nightmare. But that did not deter him, once he had got up, from devoting his morning to the laborious exercise of getting into training.

There is all around Tarascon a road planted with trees, which in the local parlance is called "*le tour de ville.*" Every Sunday, in the afternoon, the residents, who despite their imaginativeness are a regular people, always make the tour of the town, and always in the same way. Tartarin trained himself by doing it eight or ten times in the morning, and often even in the opposite direction! He proceeded with his hands behind his back, taking short steps as on a mountain, slow and sure, and the stall-keepers, horrified at this infraction of the local custom, lost themselves in speculations of the most complicated character.

At home, in his own garden, he practised leaping crevasses by jumping over the little basin wherein some water-lilies floated; on two occasions he fell in, and was obliged to go and change his clothes. These drawbacks only excited him to fresh effort, and, risking vertigo, he walked along the narrow rim of the basin, to the manifest alarm of the old servant, who could by no means understand all these performances.

At the same time he ordered from Avignon *crampons*, such as are recommended by Whymper, for his boots, and an ice-axe of the Kennedy pattern; he also procured a cooking-lamp, two waterproof coverings, and two hundred feet of rope of his own invention, twisted with iron wire.

The arrival of these different articles, the mysterious comings and goings which their manufacture necessitated, exercised the Tarasconnais very greatly. It was reported in the town that the President was preparing a *coup*. But of what nature? Something great for certain, for according to the brave and sententious commandant Bravida, a retired captain who only dealt in apophthegms, "The eagle does not hunt flies!"

With his most intimate friends Tartarin remained impenetrable; but at the club meetings they would remark the trembling of his voice and his flashing eyes when he spoke to Costecalde—an indirect result of this new expedition, of which the dangers and fatigues became more accentuated as the time drew nearer. The unlucky man did not conceal them from himself, and he looked at them in such lugubrious colours that he put his affairs in order and wrote his last wishes, the expression of which costs the Tarasconnais, who love their lives, so much that they generally die intestate!

So one morning in June, a bright, sunny day, without a cloud in the sky, the door of the study open to the neat little garden with its sanded walks, on which the exotic plants threw clearly-defined shadows, in which a tiny jet of water trickled amid the joyous cries of the Savoyards who were playing at *marelle* before the gate,—on that morning see Tartarin in slippers, and easy flannel costume,

happy, satisfied, smoking a favourite pipe, and reading aloud as he wrote:

"This is my will."

One had need to have a heart firm in its place and solidly fixed; these are cruel moments! Nevertheless, neither his hand nor his voice shook, while he devised to the citizens all the ethnographical riches treasured in his little house, carefully dusted and kept in first-rate order :

"To the Alpine Club, the baobab (*Arbos gigantea*), to be placed on the chimney-piece of the hall of science.

"To Bravida, my fowling-pieces, revolvers, hunting-knives, Malay knives, tomahawks, and other deadly weapons.

"To Excourbaniès, all my pipes, calumets, *narghilés*, and little pipes for kif and opium smoking.

"To Costecalde—yes, Costecalde himself had his legacy—the famous poisoned arrows. (Mind you don't touch them !)"

Perhaps Tartarin had a secret hope that the man would touch them and die, but no such idea was evidenced in the will, which closed with these words of divine mansuetude :

"I beg my dear Alpinists not to forget their president. I hope they will forgive my mortal enemy as I forgive him, although it is he, nevertheless, who has occasioned my death."

Here Tartarin was compelled to stop,

blinded by his tears. For one moment he seemed to see himself a mangled mass at the foot of some lofty mountain, picked up in a wheelbarrow, and his shapeless remains carried to Tarascon. Oh, power of the Provençal imagination! he was assisting at his own funeral, listening to the chants for the dead, the discourse at the grave. " Poor Tartarin! *péchère!*" And lost amid the crowd of his friends, he began to weep for himself!

But almost immediately the sight of his study, filled with sunlight, glittering with weapons and rows of pipes, the song of the little *jet d'eau* in the garden, brought him back to the reality of things. On the other hand, why should he die? why even go away? Who compelled him to do so, if not his own self-respect? To risk his life for a presidential chair and three letters!

But this was only weakness, and did not last longer than the other impression. At the end of five minutes the will was finished, signed, and sealed with an enormous black seal, and the great man then made the last preparations for his departure.

Once again Tartarin of the warren had triumphed over Tartarin of the cabbage-garden. And we might say of this Tarascon hero what was said of Turenne: "His body was not always ready to go into battle, but his soul carried him there in spite of himself."

On the evening of that very day, as the last stroke of ten was sounding from the *maison de ville*, and the streets, already deserted, were clear except for here and there a belated one knocking for admission, a gruff voice half strangled with fear cried in the dark, "Good-night, *au mouain*," and then, with a sudden closing of the door, a pedestrian glided through the darkened town where the fronts of the houses were only illuminated by the red and green tints brightly reflected from the bottles in Bézuquet's shop, which were projected with the silhouette of the chemist himself, with his elbows on his desk, and sleeping on the Codex. He indulged in a little nap every evening in this manner, from nine till ten, so that— as he said—he might be all the fresher at night should any one require his services. Between ourselves, this was a mere Tarasconnade, for no one ever called him up, and indeed he had himself severed the wire of the night-bell in order that he might sleep the more soundly.

Suddenly Tartarin entered, wrapped up, his travelling-bag in his hand, and so pale, so discomposed, that the chemist, with that vivid local imagination of which the shop did not deprive him, believed that some fearful and terrible thing had happened.

"Unhappy man!" he exclaimed, "what is

the matter? You have been poisoned? Quick, quick, the ipecacuanha!"

He was hurrying off, upsetting his bottles, when Tartarin, to stop him, was obliged to hold him round the body: "Just listen now, *què diable!*"—and in his sharp tones the spitefulness of the actor who has made a bad entrance was manifest. The chemist once again brought back to his counter by an iron hand, Tartarin whispered:

"Are we alone, Bézuquet?"

"*Bé oui!*" replied the other, looking about him in vague terror. "Pascalon has gone to bed (Pascalon was his pupil), and mother also—But why?"

"Shut your shutters," said Tartarin in a commanding tone, without replying to the question. "They can see us from outside."

Bézuquet obeyed, trembling. He was an old bachelor, living with his mother, whom he had never quitted; he was as timid and gentle as a girl, and his demeanour contrasted strangely with his swarthy face and thick lips, his immense hooked nose, which bent over his long moustache—a head of an Algerian pirate before the conquest. These antitheses are common in Tarascon, where the heads possess too much of the Roman and Saracenic character: heads with the expression of models in a school of design, unfitted to mere tradespeople and the ultra-pacific manners of the little town.

Thus it was that Excourbaniès, who had the air of one of the bold companions of Pizarro, was a mercer, and rolled flaming yellow eyes when measuring off two yards of thread; and that Bézuquet, labelling the Spanish liquorice and the *sirupus gummi*, resembled an ancient rover of the Barbary coast.

When the shutters had been closed, and fastened with bolt and bar, Tartarin said, "Listen, Ferdinand," for he had a habit of calling people by their Christian names. Then he arose and "emptied his heart," which was full of bitterness against his associates. He related the low manœuvres of "*Jambe de coq*," the trick which they wished to play him at the next election, and the manner in which he hoped to checkmate them.

In the first place, it was most important to keep the matter a secret, and not reveal it until the precise moment which would determine the success of the plan had arrived, always except in case of an accident—one of those fearful catastrophes—"*Eh! coquin de sort*, Bézuquet; don't whistle like that while I am speaking."

This was one of the chemist's little habits. Being taciturn by nature—a phenomenon in Tarascon—he gained the confidence of the President; his big lips, always like an O, preserved the habit of a continual whistling, which seemed to ridicule every one, even in the most solemn moments.

And while the hero was alluding to his possible death, and saying, as he placed the folded, sealed, packet upon the table, "My last wishes are declared here, Bézuquet: I have chosen you as the executor of my will "

"*Hu, hu, hu*," whistled the chemist, carried

away by his mania, but really very much moved, and quite appreciating the importance of the part he had to play.

Then the hour of departure approached: he wished to drink success to the enterprise —" something good, *qué?* a glass of the Garus Elixir." After many cupboards had been opened and searched, he remembered that his

mother had the keys of the Garus. It would be necessary to wake her, and tell who was there. So a substitute for the elixir was found in a glass of the syrup of Calabria, a summer beverage, modest and inoffensive, of which Bézuquet was the inventor, and which was advertised in the *Forum* as "*Sirop de Calabre*, ten sous the bottle, including a glass"! "*Sirop de Cadavre,*" that infernal Costecalde would say, for he sneered at all successes: for the rest, this abominable play upon the words only aided the sale, and the Tarasconnais were exceedingly fond of this *sirop de Cadavre*.

The libation performed, a few last words exchanged, the friends tore themselves asunder. Bézuquet was still whistling through his moustache, while great tears were rolling down his cheeks.

"Adieu, *au mouain*," said Tartarin in a rough voice, feeling as if he were about to weep also; and as the shutter of the door had been put up, the hero was obliged to leave the shop on all fours.

The trials of his journey were already commencing.

Three days later he disembarked at Vitznau, at the foot of the Rigi. As a preliminary canter to get into training for mountaineering, the Rigi attracted him because of its low altitude (1800 mètres, about ten times the height of *Mont-Terrible*, the most elevated peak of the *Alpines!*), and also because of the splendid panorama which is obtainable from the summit, all the Bernese Alps seated, white and rosy, round the lakes, waiting till the climber shall make his choice, and throw his ice-axe at one of them.

Sure of being recognised *en route*, and perhaps followed—for it was a weakness of his to fancy he was as well-known throughout France as he was celebrated and popular in Tarascon—he had made a wide *détour* to reach Switzerland, and did not "harness" himself until he had crossed the frontier. It was a good thing he did not, as his "armament" could never be contained in a French railway compartment.

But, however commodious the Swiss railway carriages may be, the Alpinist, embarrassed by implements to the use of which he was quite unaccustomed, stabbed people's toes with the point of his alpenstock, harpooned others with his *crampons*, and everywhere he went, in the railway stations, the hotels, or on the steamer, he excited as much astonishment as cursing, elbowing, and angry looks, which he could not understand, and which were torture to his candid and affectionate nature. To sum up, there was a leaden sky, heavy clouds, and a pelting rain.

It rained at Bâle, where the houses are washed and re-washed by servants and the water from heaven; it rained at Lucerne, on the quay where the mails and luggage seemed to be just recovered from a wreck; and when he reached Vitznau, on the brink of the Lake of the Four Cantons, there was the same deluge falling upon the green slopes of the Rigi, encircled by black clouds, with torrents dashing over the rocks, making cascades in dust-like spray, dropping from all the stones and from every fir-branch. Tartarin had never seen so much water before.

He entered an *auberge*, and was served

"She burst into a peal of inextinguishable laughter."

with some *café au lait*, honey, and butter, the only really good things that he had so far enjoyed in his journey. Then, once more refreshed, his beard cleared of some honey by means of a corner of his *serviette*, he made preparations to attempt his first ascent.

"And now," said he, as he was packing up his *sac*, "how long will it take me to get to the top of the Rigi?"

"An hour or an hour and a quarter, monsieur. But you must make haste; the train will start in five minutes."

"A train up the Rigi! You are joking!"

Through the leaden-sashed window of the *auberge* she showed him the train which was about to ascend. Two large covered waggons without windows, pushed by a locomotive with a short chimney and with a kettle-shaped body—a monstrous insect clinging to the mountain, and getting quite out of breath in its attempt to climb the steep sides.

The two Tartarins—the wild and the domestic species—were shocked at the idea of ascending in this hideous machine. One thought it ridiculous to climb the Alps in a lift: as for the other, the light bridges which carry the line over chasms, with the prospect of a fall of a thousand feet if the train left the metals ever so little, inspired him with all kinds of sad reflections, which found reason for the establishment of the little cemetery at Vitznau, the tombs in which are squeezed together at the bottom of the slope like the linen displayed in the courtyard of a laundry. Evidently this cemetery is established as a matter of precaution, so that in case of accident travellers may find it quite convenient.

"I'll go up on foot," said the valiant Tarasconnais. "It will give me some exercise. *Zou!*"

And so he went, very much pre-occupied by his alpenstock in the presence of the staff of the *auberge*, who ran to the door shouting to him the way, indications which he never heard. He first pursued an ascending path, paved with great pebbles, of unequal sizes, pointed, as in a Southern lane, and bordered with wooden channels to permit the escape of the rain-water.

To right and left are fine orchards, grassy

meadows crossed by these same irrigating pipes made from trunks of trees. This arrangement causes a continual splashing of water from the top to the bottom of the mountain, and every time that the ice-axe of the Alpinist caught in the low branches of an oak or chestnut his cap crackled as if subjected to a shower from a watering-pot.

"*Diou!* what a quantity of water!" sighed the man of the South. But things became worse when the paved way ceased, for then he was obliged to pick his way through the torrent, to leap from one stone to another, so as not to wet his gaiters. Then the downpour hindered him, penetrating, continuous; and it seemed to get colder as he ascended. When he stopped to take breath, he could hear nothing but the rushing of the water in which he stood, half-drowned, and when he turned round he could see the black clouds united to the lake by long fine rods of glass, through which the *chalets* of Vitznau glistened like freshly varnished toy-houses.

Several men and children passed close by,

some with heads bent down and backs curved under the hod of white wood containing supplies for some villa or *pension*, whose balconies could be perceived mid-way.

"To the Rigi-Kulm?" asked Tartarin, to assure himself that he was in the right direction; but his extraordinary equipment, and particularly the knitted comforter which shrouded his face, alarmed those he addressed, and every one of them, after staring at him with wide-open eyes, hurried upwards without replying.

These meetings soon became few and far between: the last human being he encountered, was an old woman who was washing some linen in the trunk of a tree under the shade of an enormous red umbrella fixed in the ground.

"Rigi-Kulm?" asked the Alpinist.

The old woman raised to his a terrified and idiotic face, bearing a *goitre* which hung from her neck, as large as the bell of a Swiss cow: then after having taken a long look at him she burst into a peal of inextinguishable laughter, which stretched her mouth from ear to ear, puckering up her little eyes; and every time that she opened them again, the sight of Tartarin standing before her, his ice-axe on his shoulder, seemed to redouble her mirth.

"*Tron de l'air!*" growled the Tarasconnais, "it's lucky she's a woman;" and bursting with rage he continued his *route*, losing his way in a pine wood, where his boots slipped upon the soaking moss.

Beyond that, the scene changed. No more paths, no trees nor pastures. A few mournful slopes, bare, but sustaining great boulders, which he was obliged to scale on hands and knees for fear of falling; morasses full of yellow mud, which he crossed slowly, testing the quagmire with his alpenstock, and lifting his feet like a knife-grinder. Every moment he consulted the compass which hung as a charm to his watch-chain ; but, whether owing to the altitude or to the variations of the temperature, the needle seemed defective. He had no means by which he could take his bearings, for the thick yellow fog that prevented him from seeing ten paces in any direction, was penetrated by a thick, cold sleet, which made the ascent more and more laborious.

Suddenly he halted, the ground was white in front. Take care of your eyes ! He had come to the snow-line !

Immediately he drew his glasses from their case and adjusted them firmly. The moment was a solemn one. Somewhat nervous, but proud all the same, Tartarin felt that at one bound he had ascended 3000 feet towards the peaks and their dangers !

He advanced with great precaution, thinking of the *crevasses* and the *rotures* of which he had read, and in his heart of hearts cursing the people of the *auberge*, who had advised him to ascend straight up without a guide.

Night would surprise him on the mountain.
Could he find a hut, or only the projection
of a rock, to shelter himself? Suddenly
he perceived, on the wild and desolate
platform, a kind of wooden *chalet*, bound
with a placard bearing enormous letters,
which he deciphered with difficulty: PHO---
TO GRA PHIE DU RI GI—KULM. At
the same moment the immense hotel with its
three hundred windows became visible to
him a little farther on between the great
lamps, which burned brightly in the fog.

III.

*An alarm on the Rigi.—Be cool! be cool!—
The Alpine horn.—What Tartarin found
on his looking-glass when he awoke.—
Perplexity.—He asks for a guide by
telephone.*

"*Qués aco!* Who goes there?" cried
Tartarin, listening attentively, and with eyes
wide open in the dark.

The pattering of many feet was audible in
the hotel - doors banged—sounds of puffing
blowing—cries of "Make haste!"—while out
of doors was a blowing of horns, and a rush

D

of flame lighted up the windows and the curtains.

Fire!

With a single bound Tartarin was out of bed, and, rapidly shod and dressed, gained the still gas-lit staircase, where he found, descending, a buzzing swarm of young ladies hastily *coiffées*, wrapped up in green shawls, woollen scarves—anything that first came to hand when they got out of bed.

Tartarin, with a view to fortifying his own courage, and to reassure the young ladies as he rushed about and ran against everybody, cried out, "Keep cool! keep cool!" with the voice of a sea-gull—a thin, faint voice—one of those which one hears in dreams, which give the "creeps" to the bravest of us. Can you imagine how the young ladies almost shouted with laughter as they looked at him? only thinking him very funny indeed. They had no idea of the danger—at their age!

Fortunately the old diplomatist came after them, rapidly arrayed in a dressing-gown over white *caleçons*, and silken slippers.

At last there was a man! Tartarin ran up to him gesticulating: "Ah, Monsieur le Baron, what a terrible mishap! Do you know anything about it? Where is it? How did it break out?"

"Who? what?" bleated the bewildered Baron, who understood nothing of all this.

"Why, the fire!"

"What fire?"

The unfortunate man was evidently so vacant and stupid that Tartarin left him to himself, and dashed out of doors to organise assistance.

"Assistance! Help!" repeated the Baron; and after him five or six waiters, who slept standing in the antechamber, stared at each other and repeated in a bewildered fashion, "Help!"

At the first step he took outside the building Tartarin perceived his mistake. There was not the least sign of a fire. A nipping cold, a dark night illuminated by pine-torches which threw a lurid glare upon the snow.

At the bottom of the steps, a man with an Alpine horn emitted his modulated lowings, a monotonous *ranz des vaches* of three notes, with which it is the fashion on the Rigi-Kulm to awake the sun-worshippers, and to announce to them the approaching appearance of the luminary.

It is stated that he shows himself sometimes, at his first rising, at the extreme edge of the mountain behind the hotel. To find his bearings Tartarin had only to follow the continual tittering of the girls, who were walking close to him.

But he proceeded more slowly, still feeling very sleepy, and stiff in his limbs after his six hours' climb.

"Is that you Maniloff?" asked a clear-toned voice suddenly out of the darkness—a lady's voice: "come and help me; I have lost my shoe."

Tartarin recognised the bird-like notes of his little neighbour at

"A little hand resting for a minute on his shoulder."

the *table d'hôte*, whose graceful profile he caught in the pale light reflected from the snowy ground.

"It is not Maniloff, mademoiselle; but if I can be of any assistance———"

She uttered a little cry of surprise and fear, and made a gesture of repulsion which Tartarin did not see, for he was already stooping down and tapping the short grass, which crackled with frost beneath his fingers.

"*Tè, pardi!* here it is!" he exclaimed joyfully. He shook the slender shoe, which was powdered with rime, knelt down on one knee on the cold damp ground, in the most gallant fashion, and asked that he might be rewarded by having the honour to put on Cinderella's slipper!

The lady, more unamiable than in the story, replied with a "No" very sharply uttered, and hopping on one foot endeavoured to insert her silk stocking into the reddish-brown shoe; but she would never have succeeded without the aid of our hero, who was very much pleased to feel a little hand resting for a minute on his shoulder.

"You have very good eyes," she said by way of acknowledgment, while they proceeded groping their way in the dark side by side.

"The result of sporting habits, mademoiselle."

"Ah, then you are a sportsman!"

She said this with some raillery and a little incredulity in her voice. Tartarin had only to mention his name to convince her of the fact, but, like all illustrious people, he was discreet, and, with a kind of coquetry, wished to surprise her by degrees as it were:

"I am a hunter, as a matter of fact!"

She continued in her ironical tone—

"And what game do you hunt for choice, now?"

"The large carnivora and the great deer," replied Tartarin, believing he would overwhelm her.

"Do you find many of them on the Rigi?" she asked.

Always polite in his repartee, Tartarin was going to reply that on the Rigi he had met none but *gazelles*, when his remark was cut short by the approach of two shadows who called out,

"Sonia! Sonia!"

"I am coming," she said, and then turning towards Tartarin, whose eyes, now accustomed to the obscurity, were able to distinguish her pretty pale face under a mantilla *en manola*, she added, this time seriously:

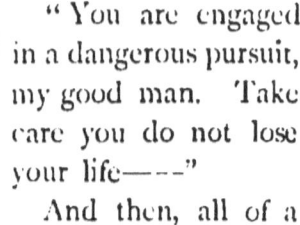

"You are engaged in a dangerous pursuit, my good man. Take care you do not lose your life——"

And then, all of a sudden, she disappeared in the darkness with her friends.

Later on the menacing import of these words occurred to the imaginative mind of the Southerner; but at the time he was only vexed at the use of the term "good man," flung at his stoutness and grey hair, and at the careless disappearance of the young lady just as he was going to tell her who he was, and to gloat over her stupefaction.

He advanced a few paces in the direction of the group who were preceding him, with a confused murmur in his ears—the coughing, the sneezing of the assembled tourists, who

were waiting with impatience the rising of the sun: some of the most adventurous climbed up into a little stand or belvedere, the supports of which, coated with snow, were distinguishable in the dying darkness of the night.

A gleam of light began to streak the eastern sky, and was saluted by another note on the Alpine horn, and with that "ah" which escapes from the overcharged bosoms of the spectators as the prompter's last bell rings for the raising of the curtain. Thin as a crack in a lid, the light gradually extended itself, widening the horizon, but at the same time raising from the valley a thick, opaque, yellow fog, which became thicker and more extended as day broke. It was like a veil between the stage and the audience.

They were obliged to give up all hope of seeing the beautiful effects described by the guide-books. On the other hand, the heterodox costumes of the dancers of the night before, hurriedly aroused from sleep, were displayed as in a magic lantern, ludicrous and eccentric; for shawls, counterpanes, even the curtains of the beds which they had occupied were worn. Beneath the varied head-dresses—silk or cotton caps, hoods, toques, night-caps—were scared, puffed faces, the heads of shipwrecked people on an island in the open sea, on the watch for a sail in the offing with all the intentness of gaze of which their widely open eyes were capable.

And nothing—all the time nothing!

Nevertheless, some of them in an access of good will made believe to distinguish the peaks from the belvedere; and the "clucking" of the Peruvian girls were heard as they surrounded a big fellow in a check ulster who was enumerating in the calmest way the invisible panoramic objects of the Bernese Alps, naming and designating, in a loud voice, the peaks which were enveloped in the fog:

"On the left you see the Finsteraarhorn, 12,825 feet high; the Schreckhorn, the Wetterhorn, the Mönch, the Jungfrau, to the elegant proportions of which I would call the attention of the young ladies."

"*Bé!* true, that fellow does not want for impudence," said Tartarin to himself. Then as an after-thought he muttered—" But I know that voice—*pas mouain.*"

He recognised the accent—that *assent* of the South of France which is as distinguishable at a distance as the garlic is; but so pre-occupied was he in following up the fair unknown that he did not stop, continuing to inspect the groups he passed. She had, no doubt, returned to the hotel, as every one else was now doing, tired of remaining shivering in the cold and stamping their feet. Some bent backs, some tartar-plaids, the ends of which swept the snow, disappeared into the ever-thickening fog! Very soon nothing remained on the plateau, cold and desolate in the grey dawn, but Tartarin, and the Alpine horn-blower who continued to extract melancholy howls from the instrument like a dog baying at the moon.

He was a little old man, with a long beard, wearing a Tyrolese hat embellished with green tassels which fell down his back, and bearing, like those of all the retainers of the hotel, the *Regina Montium* in letters of gold. Tartarin advanced towards him to bestow on him a *pour-boire,* as he had seen the other tourists do.

"Let us go to bed, old fellow," said he, tapping the man upon the shoulder with the Tarascon familiarity. "A regular humbug, *qué,* this Rigi sunrise!"

The old man continued to blow his horn.

finishing his *ritornello* with a silent laugh which wrinkled up the corners of his eyes and shook the green tassels of his hat.

Tartarin, after all, did not regret the experience of the night. The meeting with the pretty blonde made amends to him for his interrupted sleep, for although near his fiftieth year he had still a warm heart, a romantic imagination, an ardent soul. When he again had reached his bedroom, and had shut his eyes to woo sleep, he still fancied he could feel in his hand the tiny shoe, and hear the jerky appeals of the young lady: "Is that you, Maniloff?"

Sonia! What a beautiful name. She was certainly a Russian; and these young men were travelling with her—friends of her brother no doubt. Then all became misty; the golden-curled little head went to mingle with other floating and drowsy visions—the slopes of the Rigi and the waterfalls,— and very soon the heroic snoring of the great man, sonorous and rhythmical, filled the little room and a considerable section of the corridor besides.

As he was about to go down stairs next morning, at the first sound of the breakfast-bell, Tartarin was reassuring himself that his beard had been properly brushed, and that he did not look very badly in his mountaineering costume, when suddenly he began to shake with fear. Before him, open, and stuck in the looking-glass, an anonymous letter displayed the following threatening words:

"*Français du diable, thy disguise but ill conceals thee. We have spared thee this time, but if thou crossest our path again, beware!*"

Perfectly astounded, he read and re-read the note without comprehending it. Of whom, of what, was he to beware? How had the letter got there? Evidently while he slept, for he had not perceived it when he returned from his early morning promenade. He rang for the chambermaid, a flat-faced creature marked with small-pox like a Gruyère cheese, from whom he could elicit nothing intelligible except that she was of "*pon famille,*" and never entered the rooms when a gentleman was in possession.

"What a very curious thing," said Tartarin, as he turned the note over and over. He was greatly impressed. In a moment the name of Costecalde crossed his mind, Costecalde imbued with his own plans of mountaineering, and endeavouring to turn him aside by menaces and plotting! Then he began to persuade himself that the letter was a hoax, for he soon abandoned the other theory; perhaps some of the girls who had laughed at him so merrily had perpetrated it,—they were so independent, these young English and American ladies!

The second bell sounded. He put the anonymous letter in his pocket. "After all, we shall soon see," he muttered, and the

formidable *moue* which accompanied this reflection indicated the heroism of his soul.

A new surprise awaited him at the breakfast-table. Instead of the pretty little neighbour with the golden hair he perceived the vulture-like neck of an old English woman whose long "weepers" swept the cloth.

It was repeated near him that the young lady and her party had left by the early train.

"*Cré nom! je suis floué*," exclaimed the Italian tenor who the night before had declared so rudely to Tartarin that he did not understand French. He had evidently learnt it in the night!

The tenor rose from his chair, threw down his *serviette* and rushed out, leaving our hero completely dumbfounded.

A great many of the guests also

took their departure. It is always thus on the Rigi, where no one remains more than four-and twenty hours. Besides, the arrangements of the table are invariably the same, the dessert dishes in long rows separating the two factions. But that morning the Rice Party were triumphant in the large majority—reinforced by some illustrious personages; and the Prunes, as was said, did not show to advantage.

Tartarin, without taking either side, went up stairs, fastened up his knapsack, and sent for his bill. He had had quite enough of *Regina montium*, of its *table d'hôte*, and its "dummies."

Suddenly reminded of his Alpine mania by the touch of his ice-axe, the rope, and the *crampons* with which he was again accoutred, he began to burn with the desire to attack some real mountain—a peak without a lift and a photographic studio in the open. He hesitated between the more elevated Finsteraarhorn and the more celebrated Jungfrau, while the fair virginal name of the latter brought the little Russian once more to his memory.

As he was balancing these questions in his mind while his bill was being got ready, he amused himself in the large, silent, and melancholy hall, by looking at the coloured photographs on the wall, which represent the glaciers, the snow-slopes, the celebrated and dangerous passes of the mountains. Here is a party in single file, like ants in search of food, upon an ice-*arête*, steep and blue; farther on an enormous crevasse with sea-green sides, across which a ladder had been flung, and was being crossed by a lady on her knees, then by an *abbé* holding up his gown.

The mountaineer of Tarascon, resting his hands upon his ice-axe, had had no idea of such difficulties as those; but he must encounter them somehow!

Suddenly his face paled in fear.

In a black frame was an engraving after the famous picture of Gustave Doré, representing the accident on the Matterhorn. Four human bodies, on their backs or on their faces, were sliding down the snow-slope, their arms extended, their hands beating the snow, seeking the broken rope on which their lives depended, and which had only served to drag them more easily to death over the precipice when they fell pell-mell with ropes, axes, green veils, and all the pleasant apparatus of the ascent which had become so terribly tragic.

"*Mâtin!*" said Tartarin, speaking aloud in dismay.

One of the polite managers heard his exclamation, and thought it his duty to reassure the guest. Accidents of that kind were becoming more and more rare: prudence was one essential qualification, and, particularly, a good guide.

Tartarin inquired whether the manager could tell him of one in confidence. Not that he had any fear; but it was always best to be on the safe side.

The man considered the point with a very important air, caressing his whiskers the while. "In confidence? Ah! if monsieur had only mentioned it sooner we had here this morning the very man. The courier of a Peruvian family."

"He is acquainted with the mountain?" asked Tartarin with a knowing air.

"Oh, monsieur, with every mountain in Switzerland, Savoy, the Tyrol, and India, in the whole world—he has done them all; he knows them by heart, and will tell you about them. He is something like! I believe they would relinquish him without making any difficulty. With such a man as he a child could go anywhere without danger!"

"Where is he? Where can he be found?"

"At the Kaltbad, monsieur, where he is arranging the rooms for his party. We can telephone."

A telephone, on the Rigi!

That was the crowning of the edifice. Tartarin was never astonished at anything after that!

In five minutes the *garçon* returned with the reply.

The Peruvians' courier was leaving for Tellsplatte, where he would certainly stay the night.

This Tellsplatte is a memorial chapel, one of the shrines established in honour of William Tell, many of which are found in Switzerland. People go there to see the frescoes which a celebrated painter of Bâle has executed on the walls of the chapel.

It was scarcely an hour by steamboat or an hour and a half perhaps. Tartarin did not hesitate. He might thus lose a day, but he must pay his respects to William Tell, for whom he had a strong predilection; and then there was the chance to secure this wonderful guide and arrange to do the Jungfrau with him.

En route, *zou !*

He immediately paid his bill, in which the sunrise and sunset were included as well as the lights and attendance, and then, preceded by the terrible clanking of iron which disseminated fear and surprise wherever he went, he proceeded to the railway for to descend the Rigi on foot when he had already walked up it seemed to him waste of time, and would, besides, be doing too much honour to that artificial mountain.

"A detachment of the Salvation Army."

IV

On board the steamer.—Rain.—The hero of Tarascon salutes the Shades.—The truth about William Tell.—Disillusion.—Tartarin of Tarascon never existed!—" Tè! Bompard!"

HE had left snow on the Rigi-Kulm below on the lake he found rain, a fine close rain, a kind of mist in which the mountains appeared like clouds.

The *Föhn* wind was blowing, making waves upon the lake, where the gulls, flying low, seemed to be carried on by the billows: one could almost fancy one's self at sea.

Tartarin recalled his departure from

Marseilles fifteen years before, when he was setting out to hunt lions—he thought of that sky without a cloud, bathed in light; the blue sea, blue as indigo, stirred up into crisp salt waves by the mistral; the salutes of the forts, the clanging of the bells, intoxication, joy, sun, all the fairy impressions of the first voyage!

What a contrast was it with the black deck of the almost deserted little steamer, on which he made out as in a mist a few passengers wrapped in ulsters or mackintoshes; and the man at the wheel, motionless abaft, hooded, grave, and sybilline, above the legend couched in three languages: "You must not speak to the man at the wheel."

This prohibition was quite unnecessary, for no one spoke on board the *Winkelried* at all,—no more on deck than in the cabins, which were crammed with passengers of melancholy mien, sleeping, reading, yawning, pell-mell, their light baggage strewn upon the benches. They appeared like a number of people being transported on the day after a *coup d'état*.

From time to time the hoarse steam whistle announced the approach to a station. A noise of footsteps and of the unloading of luggage resounded from the deck. Then the shore faded into the mist, advanced again, displaying the dark green slopes, the villas shivering amid the saturated trees, the poplars in rows along the road, bordered all its length by sumptuous hotels designated in letters of gold on their façades—the hotels Meyer, Müller, du Lac, with numbers of heads belonging to bored residents looking out of the dripping casements.

The people crossed the gangway to the shore; descended, ascended; equally dirty, soaked, and silent. On the tiny pier a crowd of umbrellas was visible: the omnibus quickly disappeared. Then the paddle-wheels churned the water into foam and the shore receded, fading into the blurred landscape with the *pensions* Meyer, Müller, du Lac,—all the windows of which, for an instant open, displaying at every story a waving of pocket handkerchiefs, and outstretched arms, as if to say: "Have mercy!

—pity us! take us away—if you only knew—!"

Sometimes the *Winkelried* would pass another steamer, with its name in black letters on the white ground—*Germania, Guillaume Tell*. There was the same lugubrious deck, the same shiny waterproofs, the same lament-

able passage, no matter in which direction the phantom vessel was proceeding, the same distressful glances were exchanged from one to the other.

And to think that all these people were travelling for pleasure! that they were prisoners for their own pleasure in the *pensions* of Meyer, Müller, and du Lac!

Here, as at the Rigi-Kulm, the great

grievance of Tartarin, which irritated him more than the cold rain or the leaden sky, was the impossibility of speaking!

Below, he had again found some well-known faces—the member of the Jockey Club, with his niece! The Academician, Astier-Réhu, and Professor Schwanthaler, those two implacable foes, condemned to exist side by side

for a month, bound to the same itinerary, to a Cook's circular tour, with others too: but none of these illustrious Prunes would recognise the Tarasconnais, who was nevertheless easily recognisable by his comforter and his equipment, in a most indubitable manner. Every one seemed ashamed of that dance the evening before, and of the inexplicable transports into which they had been inveigled by that fat man.

Madame Schwanthaler alone came towards her partner, with the bright and rosy appearance of a little chubby fairy, and holding her skirt between two fingers as if she was about to perform a minuet, she said, "*Ballir,—dantsir,—très choli!*" Was she invoking memory, or tempting him to tread another measure? She would not let him alone; and Tartarin, to escape her importunity, went on deck again, preferring to be wet to his very bones rather than be made a laughing-stock.

And it did come down, and the sky was murky! To heighten the gloom, a whole detachment of the Salvation Army was going to Beckenried—a dozen fat girls of heavy mien, with navy-blue dresses, and coal-scuttle bonnets, under enormous red umbrellas, singing hymns, which were accompanied on the accordion by a man with wild eyes, lanky, emaciated—a kind of David Gamm. These shrill voices, spiritless and discordant as the cries of a gull, came dragging through the rain, and the smoke of the steamer which the wind beat back. Tartarin had never heard anything so deplorable in his life.

At Brunnen the detachment quitted the boat, leaving the tourists' pockets full of pious tracts; and almost immediately the accordion and the singing of these poor *larvæ* had ceased, the sky began to clear, and bits of blue became visible.

Now the steamer was entering the Bay of Uri, shaded and inclosed between wild and lofty mountains; and on the right, at the foot of Seelisberg, the tourists were shown the Grütli, where Melchtal, Fürst, and Stauffacher took the oath to deliver their land from the oppressor.

Tartarin, very much affected, reverently removed his cap, without noticing the astonishment his action aroused; he even waved his head-covering in the air three times, by way of doing homage to the *manes* of the heroes. Some passengers mistook his enthusiasm, and politely returned his salute.

At length the engine uttered a hoarse bellow, which echoed across the narrow bay. The placard which they display on deck at every landing-place—as is done at public balls at every change of dance—announced Tellsplatte. They had arrived!

The chapel is situated five minutes' walk from the landing-place, quite on the margin of the lake, on the very rock upon which William Tell leaped from Gesler's boat in the storm. Tartarin experienced a delicious emotion, while he followed the Cook's tourists along the lake, as he trod the historic ground, and recalled, and lived over again, the principal events of the great drama, the details of which he knew as well as those in his own life.

From his earliest years, William Tell had been his ideal! When, at the chemist's, (at Bézuquet's) they used to write their "likes and dislikes," their favourite poet, author, tree, scent, hero or heroine, one of the papers invariably bore the following:

"The favourite tree?—The baobab.

"The favourite scent?—Of powder.

"The favourite author?—Fenimore Cooper.

"Who would you wish to have been?—William Tell."

Tartarin on the Alps

Then in the surgery there was only one opinion—they all cried with one voice, "That is Tartarin!"

Ask yourself, then, whether he was not happy, if his heart did not beat high, when he reached this memorial chapel erected as a mark of the gratitude of the entire nation.

It seemed to him that William Tell in person, still dripping with water after his plunge in the lake, his cross-bow and arrows in his hand, would open the door to him.

"No admission. I am at work : this is not the day," shouted a voice from the interior, the tone being much increased in volume by the vaulted roof.

"Monsieur Astier-Réhu, of the French Academy."

"Herr Doctor Professor Schwanthaler."

"Tartarin de Tarascon!"

In the ogive window above the door, the artist, perched on a scaffolding, appeared in his working blouse, palette in hand.

"My *famulus* is going down to open the door to you, gentlemen," he said respectfully.

"I was sure of it," thought Tartarin. "I had only to mention my name!"

Nevertheless he had the good taste to keep back, and modestly enter after every one else.

The painter, a very fine young fellow, showing a golden head of an artist of the Renaissance, received his visitors on the wooden steps which ascended to the temporary staging erected for the painting of the chapel. The frescoes, representing the principal episodes in the life of William Tell, had been completed, all but one—the representation of the shooting at the apple in the market-place of Altorf. He was working at it then, and his young assistant *famulus*, as he called him— his hair *à l'archange*, his legs and feet bare, beneath a smock frock of the middle ages, was posing as the son of William Tell.

All these archaic personages,—red, green, yellow, blue,—of more than human stature, in narrow streets, and intended to be seen from a distance, impressed the spectators rather tamely; but they were there to admire, and they did so. Besides, nobody there knew anything about them!

"I call that most characteristic," said the pontifical Astier-Réhu, bag in hand.

And Schwanthaler, a camp-stool under his arm, not to be outdone, quoted two verses of Schiller, half of which remained in his flowing beard. Then the ladies exclaimed their delight, and for à while nothing was to be heard but such phrases as—

"*Schön! oh, schön!*"

"Yes; lovely!"

"*Exquis! délicieux!*"

One could have fancied one's self at a confectioner's!

Suddenly, a voice rang out like a trumpet blast in the silence which succeeded.

"That shoulder is wrong, I tell you: that cross-bow is out of drawing!"

We can picture the stupor of the artist, face to face with the critical mountaineer, who, with his staff in hand and ice-axe on his shoulder threatening to wound some one at every movement, was demonstrating ener-

getically that the attitude of William Tell was not correctly represented.

"And I know what I am talking about, *au mouains.'* I beg you to believe——"

"Who are you?"

"Who am I!" exclaimed Tartarin, very much "put out." Was it not for him that admission had been granted! Therefore, drawing himself up, he said: "Go and ask my name of the panthers of Zaccar, from the lions of the Atlas. *They* will perhaps inform you!"

There was a simultaneous recoil, a general alarm, at these words.

"But," asked the artist, at length, "in what way is my position not correct?"

"Look at me—you!"

Falling into position with a stamping which drove the dust from the staging in clouds, Tartarin shouldered his alpenstock after the manner of a cross-bow, and stood in position.

"Splendid! He is right. Don't stir."

Then the artist, addressing his *famulus*, cried, "Quick — a sheet of paper — a charcoal-pencil."

Tartarin was going to be painted as he stood, a dumpy, round-backed man, wrapped in his muffler to the chin; fixing the terrified *famulus* with his flaming little eye.

Imagination, oh what magic power you possess! He believed himself standing in the market-place of Altorf, facing his son— he who had never had one—a bolt in his cross-bow, another in his girdle to pierce the heart of the tyrant. More than that, he communicated the conviction to the spectators!

"It is William Tell himself!" said the artist, who, seated on a stool, was wielding his pencil in feverish haste. "Ah, monsieur, I wish I had known you sooner! You would have served for my model."

"Really! You see some resemblance, then?" asked Tartarin, feeling much flattered, but without disarranging his *pose*.

Yes, it was quite thus that the artist had pictured the hero.

"His head, too?" asked Tartarin.

"Oh, the head does not matter," replied the artist, as he stepped back to criticise his sketch. "A manly, energetic face is all that is necessary, since no one knows what William Tell was like—he probably never lived."

Tartarin let fall his "stock" in a kind of stupefaction.

"*Outre!*[1] Never lived! What is that you tell me?"

"Ask these gentlemen."

Astier-Réhu, very solemn, his three chins resting upon his white neckcloth, replied: "It is a Danish legend."

"Ice-landic," affirmed Schwanthaler, no less majestically.

"Saxo Grammaticus relates that a valiant named Tobe or Paltanoke——"

"It is written in the Viking's Saga——"

Then they proceeded, together—

"fut condamné par le roi de Danemark, Harold aux dents bleues——"

"dass der Isländische König Necding——"

With fixed eyes, extended arms, without either looking at or understanding each other,

---

[1] *Outre* and *boufre* are Tarasconnais oaths of mysterious etymology. Ladies use them at times with a softening addition—as, "*Outre! que vous me feriez dire!*"

they both spoke at the same time, as if "in the chair," in the dictatorial despotic tones of the professor assured of not being contradicted. They became excited, shouting names and dates: "Justinger de Berne!" "Jean de Winterthur!"

By and by the discussion became general, animated, furious; they brandished campstools, umbrellas, valises, while the unhappy artist went from one to another endeavouring to restore harmony, while trembling for the solidity of his staging. When the storm had ceased, he was desirous to resume his sketch,

"Fixing the terrified *famulus* with his glaring eye."

and sought the mysterious mountaineer; he of whom the panthers of Zaccar, and the lions of the Atlas could alone pronounce the name! But the Alpinist had disappeared!

He was striding furiously along through the birches and beeches, towards the hotel of Tellsplatte where the Peruvians' courier was to pass the night; and, smarting under the blow which had disillusioned him, he spoke aloud, driving his alpenstock furiously into the soaked pathway.

"Never lived! William Tell! William Tell a myth, a legend! And it is the painter intrusted with the decoration of Tellsplatte who calmly says that!" He inveighed against it as a sacrilege; he was angry with the *savants*, with this sceptical century, the impious upsetter, which respects nothing—neither glory nor beauty: "*coquin de sort!*"

Thus two hundred or three hundred years hence, when people speak of Tartarin, they will find Astier-Réhus and Schwanthalers to support the argument that no such person as Tartarin ever lived! that he was a Provençal or Barbary myth! He stopped, suffocated by his indignation—and the steep ascent; and seated himself upon a rustic bench.

From that place one can see, between the branches of the trees, the lake, and the white walls of the chapel like a new mausoleum. A blowing-off of steam and a rattling of a gangway indicated a new access of visitors. They were grouped on the shore of the lake, guide-book in hand, advancing and gesticulating as they read the legend. And suddenly, by a quick revulsion of thought, the comic side of the question came into Tartarin's head.

He thought of all historic Switzerland living upon this imaginary hero; raising statues and building chapels in his honour in the market-places of little towns and in the museums of great ones; organising patriotic *fêtes* at which people from all the cantons appear with banners carried before them; the banquets, the toasts, the speeches, the cheering, the singing, the tears which swell the manly bosoms—all this for a great patriot who, everybody knows, never had any existence!

Talk of Tarascon! Here was a *Tarasconnade* which never had its equal there!

Restored to good humour, Tartarin in a few good jumps regained the high road to Fluelen, on which stands the Tellsplatte hotel with its long green-shuttered *façade*. While waiting the announcement of dinner, the boarders were walking up and down before a rock-work cascade upon the ravined road, along which a number of unhorsed carriages were placed amid the copper-coloured pools of water.

Tartarin ascertained that the man he sought was there. He learnt that he was at dinner. "Lead me to him, *zou*," and he said it with such an authoritative air, that, notwithstanding the respectful repugnance to disturb so important a personage which was displayed, a female servant led the Alpinist through the hotel, where his appearance created some sensation, towards the precious courier who was eating by himself in a small room opening from the courtyard.

"Monsieur," began Tartarin, as he came in, ice-axe on shoulder. "Excuse me if - "

He stopped in surprise; while the courier, the lanky courier, his *serviette* tucked under his chin amid the savoury steam of a plateful of soup, let his spoon fall.

"*Vé!* Monsieur Tartarin."

"*Té!* Bompard."

It was Bompard, the former manager of the club: a good fellow enough, but afflicted with a vivid imagination which prevented him from uttering a single word of truth, an attribute which had gained for him in Tarascon the surname of the Impostor. Designated at Tarascon as an impostor, you may judge what he was! And this man was the incomparable guide, the climber of the Alps, the Himalayas, the Mountains of the Moon!

"Oh, then I understand!" exclaimed Tartarin, somewhat disappointed, but pleased, nevertheless, at finding a countryman, and hearing the dear delicious *accent du Cours*.

"*Différemment*, Monsieur Tartarin, you will dine with me, *qué?*"

Tartarin at once accepted, relishing the idea of seating himself at a nice little table laid for two, without any partisan dishes, to be able to drink freely, to talk while he ate, and to enjoy many excellent courses; for *MM. les Courriers* are very well treated by inn-keepers; they dine apart, and have the best wines and the "extra" dishes.

And there was plenty of *au moins, pas moins*, and *différemment* then!

"So it was you, *mon bon*, whom I heard in the early morning holding forth on the staging on the Rigi?"

"Eh, *parfaitemain!* I was pointing out the beauties to the young ladies. Is not the sunrise on the Alps magnificent?"

"*Superbe!*" assented Tartarin, at first without

conviction, not wishing to contradict his friend, but wound up after a minute or so ; and then it was perfectly bewildering to listen to the two Tarasconnais recalling with enthusiasm the splendours they had seen on the Rigi. It was like Joanne alternated with Bædeker!

Then, in proportion as the meal progressed, the conversation became of a more personal character—full of confidences, gush, protestations, which brought tears into the brilliant Provençal eyes, always retaining in their facile emotion a trace of farce or raillery. This was the only point in which the friends resembled each other: one so dry, salted, tanned, seamed with those peculiar professional wrinkles; the other short, broad-backed, of a sleek appearance, and of fresh complexion.

He had seen so much of it, had this poor Bompard, since he had left the club ; that insatiable imagination, which prevented him from retaining any situation, had sent him wandering under so many suns with varied fortune! And he related his adventures, enumerating all the excellent opportunities he had had of enriching himself, such as his latest invention for reducing the amount of the Army Estimates by economising the expense of *godillots*. "Do you know how? Oh, *mon Dieu*, it is very simple—by shoeing the soldiers' feet with iron."

"*Outre!*" remarked Tartarin, astonished.

Bompard continued, calm as ever, with that cool, innocent air of his:

"A grand idea, was it not? Eh! *hé*, to the War Office—but they never took any notice of me. Ah, my poor Monsieur Tartarin, I have had my bad days. I have eaten the bread of affliction before I entered the service of the Company——"

"The Company?"

Bompard discreetly lowered his voice.

"*Chut!* by and by not here!" Then resuming his natural tone, he continued: "And now, what have you all been about at Tarascon? You haven't told me anything of your reasons for coming amid the mountains."

This was the opportunity for Tartarin to unbosom himself. Without anger, but with that melancholy cadence, that *ennui*, which all great artists, beautiful women, and great conquerors of people and hearts, attain when they grow old, he related the defection of his compatriots, the plot that was being concocted to deprive him of the presidency of the club, and the decision he had come to to do some

thing heroic; to make a grand ascent, to plant the banner of Tarascon higher than it had ever yet been fixed—in fine, to prove to the Alpinists of Tarascon that he was ever worthy, always worthy—— Emotion made him pause; he was obliged to cease speaking; then:

"You know me, Gonzague!" he cried

No one could do justice to the effusiveness, the tenderness, which he threw into this troubadour-like name of Bompard. It was a kind of hand-pressing—of clasping him to his heart. "You know me, *qué!* You know whether I have ever quailed when in quest of the lion; and during the war, when we organised the defence of the club—"

Bompard nodded his head with dreadful mimicry; he could fancy himself there still.

"Well, *mon bon*, what the lions, what the Krupp guns, could not do, the Alps have done! I am afraid!"

"Don't say that, Tartarin!"

"Why not?" said the hero, with touching simplicity. "I say I am afraid, because I am!"

Then quietly, without any attitudinising, he avowed the impression which the engraving from Doré's picture had made upon him,—the catastrophe upon the Matterhorn still haunted him. He was afraid of encountering like perils, and so, hearing of a most extraordinary guide, capable of avoiding such dangers, he had come to confide in him

Then in the most matter-of-course tone he added :

"You never have been a guide, have you, Gonzague ?"

"*Hé!* yes ;" replied Bompard, smiling. "Only I have not done all I said I had."

"Of course," assented Tartarin.

Then his companion said between his teeth :

"Let us go out into the road, we shall be able to converse more freely there."

Night was coming on : a cool humid breeze was driving the black clouds across the sky wherein the setting sun had left a gleam of dusky grey. They went side by side in the direction of Fluelen, passing mute shadows of famished tourists' who were returning to the hotel, shades themselves, not uttering a word, until they reached the long tunnel through which the road is carried, and which opens here and there in "bays," terrace-fashion, over the lake.

"Let us halt here," said Bompard, whose loud voice echoed in the archway like a cannon. Then, seated on the parapet, they contemplated the beautiful view of the lake, the slopes of firs, beeches, black and thick, in the foreground ; the indistinct summits of the higher mountains, then others higher still in a confused bluish mass, like clouds ; in the middle a white line, scarcely visible, of some glacier frozen into the crevices, which was suddenly illuminated with party-coloured fires, yellow, red, and green. The mountain was being illuminated with Bengal lights.

From Fluelen rockets were sent up, breaking into multi-coloured stars, while Venetian lanterns shone and passed to and fro upon the lake in the invisible boats, carrying musicians and those assisting in the *fête*.

A truly fairy scene it was, framed in the cold, smooth granite of the tunnel walls.

"What a queer country this Switzerland is!" exclaimed Tartarin.

Bompard began to laugh.

"Ah, *vaï!* Switzerland! In the first place there is nothing Swiss in it!"

V

Confidences in a tunnel.

"SWITZERLAND at the present time, *té!* Monsieur Tartarin, is nothing more than an immense Kursaal, which is open from June till September a panoramic casino, to which people crowd for amusement, from all parts of the world; and which a tremendously wealthy company possessed of thousands of millions, which has its head-quarters in Geneva, has *exploited*. Money is necessary, you may depend, to farm, harrow, and top dress all this land, its lakes, forests, mountains, and waterfalls, to keep up a staff of *employés*, of supernumeraries, and to build upon all high places monster hotels with gas, telegraphs, and telephones all laid on."

"That is true enough," murmured Tartarin, who recalled the Rigi.

"Yes, it is true; but you have seen nothing of it yet. When you penetrate a little farther into the country, you will not find a corner which is not fixed up and machined like the floor beneath the stage in the Opera: waterfalls lighted up, turnstiles at the entrances of glaciers, and, for ascents of mountains, railways—either hydraulic or funicular. The Company, ever mindful of its clients, the English and American climbers, takes care that some famous mountains, such as the Jungfrau and the Finsteraarhorn, shall always retain their difficult and dangerous aspects, although in reality they are no more dangerous than any others."

"But, my dear fellow, the crevasses! Those horrible crevasses! If you tumble into one of them?"

"You tumble on snow, Monsieur Tartarin,

and you will come to no harm: there is always at the bottom a porter—a *chasseur*—somebody who is able to assist you up again, who will brush your clothes, shake off the snow, and respectfully inquire whether 'Monsieur has any luggage?'"

"Whatever is all this you are saying, Gonzague?"

Bompard became twice as serious as before:

"The keeping up of the crevasses is one of the greatest sources of the Company's expenditure," he replied.

There was a momentary silence in the tunnel: the surroundings were calm and peaceful. No more coloured fires, rockets, or boats on the water; but the moon had risen, and displayed another conventional scene, blue, and liquid, with edges of impenetrable shade.

Tartarin hesitated to believe his companion's mere statement. Nevertheless, he reflected upon all the curious things he had seen in four days: the sun of the Rigi; the farce of William Tell: and the inventions of Bompard seemed to him all the more credible, inasmuch as in every Tarasconnais the faculty of cramming doubles that of swallowing.

"Well, but, my good friend, how do you explain those terrible accidents – that on the Matterhorn, for instance?"

"That was sixteen years ago: the Company was not then in existence, Monsieur Tartarin."

"But only last year there was that accident on the Wetterhorn—two guides were buried with the travellers."

"That must happen sometimes, as a bait for Alpine climbers. The English would not care for a mountain which did not give them the chance of a broken head. The Wetterhorn was going down in people's estimation; but after this little accident the receipts went up immediately."

"Well, but the two guides?"

"They got out, as well as the tourists; but they were obliged to—to disappear—to be maintained abroad for six months. This was a serious expense to the Company; but it is rich enough to stand it."

"Listen, Gonzague."

Tartarin rose, one hand laid on the shoulder of the quondam manager:

"You do not wish me to come to any harm, *qué?* Well then, tell me frankly: you know my 'form' as a mountaineer—it is but middling."

"Very middling, certainly!"

"Nevertheless, do you think that I can without too great risk attempt the ascent of the Jungfrau?"

"I will answer for it, Monsieur Tartarin,

'with my head in the fire.' You have only to trust yourself to your guide."

" And suppose I get giddy ? "

" Shut your eyes."

" If I slip ? "

" Let yourself slip. It is just like the theatre. Everything is *practicable*. You run no risk."

" Ah, if I only had you there to tell me all that to repeat it to me ! *Allons*, my brave fellow — a good idea. Come with me ! "

Bompard would have asked for nothing better ; but he had his Peruvians in tow till the end of the season ; and how astonished his friend was to see him performing the services of a courier a servant !

" What would you have, Monsieur Tartarin ? The Company has the right to employ us as it seems good to them."

Then he began to reckon off on his fingers the various situations he had filled during the past three years: guide in the Oberland ; horn-player in the Alps ; an old chamois-hunter ; an old soldier of Charles X. ; Protestant pastor on the mountains——

"*Quès aco?*" asked Tartarin, in surprise. And the other in his calm way replied:

"*Bé! oui.* When you travel in German Switzerland, you may often perceive a pastor in the open air standing on a rock, or on a rustic chair, or on the trunk of a tree. Some shepherds and cheese-makers, with their caps in their hands, and women, habited in the cantonal costume, are grouped around in picturesque attitudes: the country is pretty, the pastures are green or freshly reaped; there are waterfalls along the road; and the cattle, with their heavy bells tinkling, are on all the mountain-slopes. All this, *vé!* is just decoration — puppet-show! The *employés* of the Company—guides, pastors, couriers, hotel-keepers—only are in the secret; and it is their interest not to publish it, for fear of frightening away their customers."

The Alpinist remained astounded, silent, the greatest sign of stupefaction in him. In his heart, any doubt of Bompard's veracity which he had was now removed; he was more calm concerning Alpine ascents, and the conversation soon made him joyous. The friends talked of Tarascon, of their pleasant jokes in the past when they were younger.

"Talking of jokes," said Tartarin suddenly, "they played me a nice trick at the Rigi-Kulm. Just imagine, this morning—" Then he proceeded to relate the incident of the letter fixed to his glass, which began with the emphatic *Français du diable*." "That is a mystery, *qué?*

"Who can say? perhaps—" began Bompard, who seemed to take the incident more seriously. He inquired whether Tartarin during his stay at the Kulm had any conversation with any one, and let fall a word too much.

"Ah! *vaï*, a word too much! How could one even open his mouth with all those English and Germans as mute as fishes by way of being in 'good form'!"

On reflection, however, he remembered having "given a clincher" pretty smartly to a sort of Cossack, a certain Mi–Milanoff!

"Maniloff," said Bompard, correcting him.

"You know him, then? Between you and me, I believe that this Maniloff was annoyed with me on account of a little Russian girl."

"Yes, Sonia;" murmured Bompard.

"You know her also? Ah, my friend, what a pearl of price —what a dear little grey partridge she is!"

"Sonia de Wassilief! 'Twas she who shot General Felianine dead in the open street. He was president of the court-martial which had condemned her brother to transportation for life."

Sonia an assassin! that child! that little blonde! Tartarin could not believe it.

But Bompard was precise, and gave him the details of the incident, which were well known. For two years, it appeared, Sonia had lived at Zurich, where her brother Boris, who had escaped from Siberia, had joined her. He was consumptive, and all the summer she carried him about in the bracing mountain air. The courier had frequently met them in the company of friends, who were all exiles—conspirators. The Wassiliefs, very intelligent, very energetic, still possessing some means, were at the head of the Nihilist party, with Bolibine, the assassin of the Prefect of Police, and this Maniloff, who the year before had blown up the Winter Palace.

"*Boufre!*" ejaculated Tartarin, "one has queer neighbours on the Rigi."

But there was yet another thing! Bompard was of opinion that the famous letter had come from these young people: he recognised in this the Nihilist mode of proceeding. The Czar every morning found such menaces in his own room; beneath his *serviette*.

"But," said Tartarin, who had become very pale, "why do they send them to me? What have *I* done?"

Bompard thought they must have taken him for a spy.

"A spy! I?"

"*Bé*, yes." In all the Nihilist centres—at

Zurich, Lausanne, Geneva—the Russian Government maintained at great cost a number of detectives; some time back she had enlisted the former chief of the French Imperial police with a dozen Corsicans, who followed and watched all exiled Russians, adopting a thousand disguises to entrap them. The costume of our Alpine climber, his spectacles, his accent, they had no doubt mistaken for the disguise of one of these agents.

"*Coquin de sort!* You have given me an idea," said Tartarin. "They had all the time at their heels an Italian tenor. He is a detective, you may be sure! But what am I to do now?"

"First of all, take care that you do not cross the path of these people, who have warned you that evil will befall you."

"Ah! *vai*, evil! The first of them who approaches me will get a bullet in his brain!"

And in the obscurity of the tunnel the eyes of the Tarasconnais gleamed. But Bompard, less assured than he, knew that the hatred of these Nihilists was terrible, and overtakes one secretly by underhand plotting. One had better be a rabbit like the president. You must be distrustful of the bed at the inn in which you sleep; the chair you sit upon; of the rail of the steamer, which will suddenly give way, and cause a fatal accident. And the poisoned dishes, and water!

"Beware of the spirits in your flask; of the foaming milk which is brought to you by the cowherd in *sabots*. These people stick at nothing, I can tell you!"

"Then what is left? I am a lost man!" groaned Tartarin; and, seizing the hand of his companion, he said:

"Advise me, Gonzague."

After a moment's reflection, Bompard traced out his programme. Let him depart early next morning, cross the lake, and the Pass of the Brunig, and sleep at Interlachen. The next day go up to Grindelwald by the Little Scheideck. The day after that, the Jungfrau! Then away to Tarascon, without losing an hour, without even looking back!

"I will start to-morrow, Gonzague," said our hero, in a stout voice, but with an uneasy glance around into the darkness.

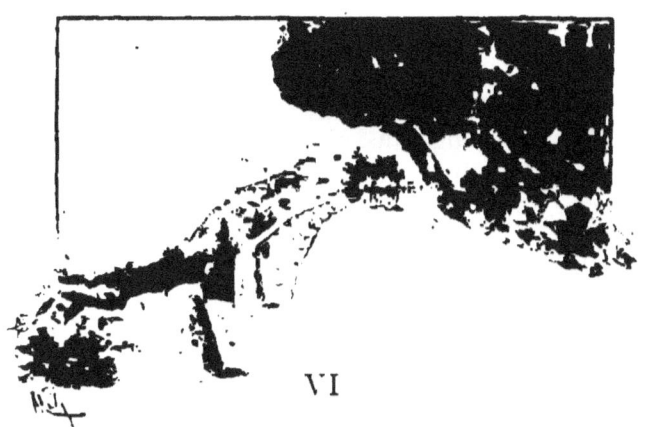

VI

The Pass of the Brünig.—Tartarin falls into the hands of the Nihilists.—Disappearance of an Italian tenor and an Avignon rope.—New exploits of a "chasseur de casquettes."—Pan! pan!

"Now then, get in! Get in!"

"But where? Where the devil am I to get in? all the places are filled! They won't have me anywhere!"

This conversation took place at the end of the Lake of the Four Cantons, at Alpnach— on that damp, undrained shore, like a delta, whence the diligences and post-carriages start in line for the Brünig Pass.

A fine, needle-pointed rain had been falling since morning, and the worthy Tartarin, impeded by his equipment, hustled about by the porters and the custom-house people, was running from carriage to carriage, noisy, and encumbered like the one-man orchestra at *fêtes*, who at every movement plays a triangle, a big drum, a Chinese hat, and cymbals. At every door our hero was saluted with cries of alarm, and the same " Full " which warned him off in all languages, the same extension motions in order to occupy as much space as possible, and to prevent the entry of such a dangerous and loud-voiced companion.

The unfortunate man perspired and panted, responded by cries of " *Coquin de bon sort*," and by despairing gestures to the impatient clamour of the convoy : " *En route ;* " " All right ; " " *Andiamo ;* " " *Vorwärtz.*" The horses pawed the ground, the drivers swore. At length the mail-guard ; an immense red-faced man in a tunic and flat cap, interfered ; and opening the door of a half-covered landau pushed Tartarin in like a parcel, and then stood upright and majestic before the splash-board, his large hand extended for a *trinkgeld*.

Humiliated, furious with the people in the carriage, who received him *manu militari*, Tartarin pretended not to look at them, thrust his purse down into his pocket, wedging in his ice-axe beside him with evident ill-humour.

"*Bonjour, monsieur*," said a sweet and well-known voice.

He looked up, and remained transfixed with terror; opposite to him was the pretty, rosy, round face of Sonia, who was seated under the hood of the landau, and also a great boy wrapped up in shawls and rugs, of whom nothing could be seen but a forehead of livid pallor and some curly hair, thin and golden as the frames of his eye-glasses. The brother, no doubt. A third person, whom Tartarin knew too well, accompanied them; this was Maniloff, the incendiary of the Winter Palace.

Sonia! Maniloff! what a trap he had fallen into!

Now they would carry out their threat in the precipitous Pass of the Brünig, flanked by deep abysses! And our hero, in one of those lightning-flashes of imagination, saw himself stretched on the pebbles in some ravine, or balanced on the high branches of an oak-tree. Fly? Whither? How? At

that moment the carriages were beginning to file off at the sound of a horn; a crowd of *gamins* presented bunches of *edelweiss* at the doors. Tartarin, in his infatuation, had a great mind to commence the attack, by spitting, with a blow of his alpenstock, the Cossack who was seated next to him: then, on reflection, he thought it more prudent to refrain. Evidently these people would not make their attack until they had gone some distance, in the uninhabited districts; and perhaps he would have an opportunity of getting out first. Besides, their intentions did not appear to him hostile. Sonia smiled on him sweetly with her pretty turquoise-blue eyes; the

big, pale young man looked at him as if interested; and Maniloff, very much softened in manner, obligingly moved up so as to permit Tartarin to put his knapsack between them. Had they discovered their mistake after reading in the register of the Rigi-Kulm Hotel the illustrious name of Tartarin of Tarascon? He wished to assure himself of this, and in a familiar, good-natured way he began:

"Delighted to meet you again, young lady; allow me to introduce myself: you are unaware with whom you have to do, while I know perfectly well who you are."

"*Chut!*" said the smiling Sonia from behind the tip of her *gant de Suède;* and she pointed to the coach-box, where, by the side of the driver, was the tenor with the sleeve-links, and the other young Russian, sheltering under the same umbrella, laughing and talking together in Italian.

Between the policemen and the Nihilists Tartarin did not hesitate.

"Do you know who that man is?" he asked in a low voice, putting his face very close to the rosy complexion of Sonia, and seeing himself reflected in her bright eyes, which grew stern and hard in their expression as she answered "Yes," with quivering lashes.

The hero shivered, but as at a theatre, with that delicious sensation in the epidermis which seizes you when the action is strong, and you sit back in your stall to see and hear better. Personally out of the business, delivered from the horrible visions which had haunted him all night, which had prevented his enjoying his coffee, butter, and honey, and, on the boat, had kept him far from the bulwarks, he now breathed freely, found life pleasant, and this little Russian irresistibly charming in her travelling *toque*, her jersey high to her neck, clinging to her arms and moulding her still slim but elegant figure. And such a child! a child in the openness of her laugh, the softness of her cheeks, and the pretty grace with which she spread her shawl over her brother's knees, asking him if he were well and not cold. How could one believe that that little hand, so slender in its chamois glove, had had the moral force and physical courage to kill a man!

Nor did the others appear ferocious either. All had the same ingenuous laugh—a little sad and constrained on the lips of the invalid, more noisy in the case of Maniloff, who, very youthful under his shaggy beard, would explode, like a schoolboy out for a holiday, in roars of exuberant merriment.

The third companion, he whom they called

Bolibine, and who was chatting with the Italian, was as much amused, and would often turn round to translate the tales which the pretended singer related of his successes at the St. Petersburg Opera-house; his *bonnes fortunes*, the sleeve-links which lady subscribers had presented to him on his departure; the curious buttons, graven with the three notes *la, do, re, (l'adoré)*; and this pun, repeated in the landau, caused such amusement that the tenor drew himself up proudly, and twirled his moustache with such a "killing" air as he stared at Sonia, that Tartarin began to ask himself whether he had not to do with ordinary tourists, and a real tenor!

But the carriages, driving rapidly, rolled over the bridges, and alongside the pretty lakes, the flowery meads, the lovely orchards, dripping and deserted, for it was Sunday, and the peasants were dressed in their holiday garments, the women wearing long plaits of hair and silver chains. The travellers were beginning to ascend the zig-zag road amid the woods of oak and beech; by degrees the magnificent horizon unrolled itself on the left hand; and at each turn of the carriage, streams, and valleys, from which uprose church steeples, were seen; and in the distance the snowy peak of the Finsteraarhorn sparkled in the beams of the invisible sun.

After a while the road became shaded,

and of a wilder aspect. On one side was gloomy shadow, a chaos of trees planted on the slope, twisted and irregular, amongst which the splashing of a torrent was audible: on the right an immense rock overhung the path, bristling with branches which sprung from the crevices in its sides.

They were not laughing in the landau now:

all were admiring the scenery, and with uplifted faces endeavouring to catch sight of the top of the granite tunnel.

"One would almost imagine we were in the forests of the Atlas," remarked Tartarin gravely, and his speech passing unnoticed he added—"Without the roaring of the lions, of course."

"You have heard them then, monsieur?" inquired Sonia.

Heard lions! He! Then, with an indulgent smile, he replied: "I am Tartarin of Tarascon, mademoiselle."

Now see what barbarians they were! If he had said "I am called Dupont," it would have been just the same. They were unacquainted with the name of Tartarin!

However, he did not feel vexed, and replied to the question of the young lady as to whether the roar of the lion frightened him: "No, mademoiselle; my camel trembled greatly as I rode him, but I visited my bait as quietly as if in the neighbourhood of a herd of cows. At a distance, the roar is something like this——"

With a view to give Sonia an exact idea of the thing, he forced from his chest in his most sonorous tones a most formidable "*Meuh,*" which rose, extending in volume, and was reflected back by the echo of the rock. The horses pranced, the travellers in all the carriages stood up, greatly alarmed, wanting to know what had happened, and the cause of such an awful noise ; then recognising the Alpinist, whose capped head and voluminous equipment were visible over the hood of the landau, they asked themselves once more : " What can that creature be ? "

He himself, perfectly calm, continued to illustrate the details, the manner of attacking the beast, the conquest, and the despatching of it, the diamond "sight" with which his gun was supplied so as to enable him to fire straight at night. The young girl listened, bending towards him, with the greatest attention, as evidenced by the slight palpitation of her nostrils.

"'They say that Bombonnel still hunts," said her brother. " Did you know him ? "

" Yes," replied Tartarin, without enthusiasm. "He is by no means unskilful. But we have better than he."

A word to the wise! Then in a melancholy tone he continued: "After all, one's greatest pleasures are in hunting noble game. When one cannot get that life seems void, and one does not know how to fill up existence."

At this juncture, Maniloff, who understood French although he did not speak it, seemed to listen intently to Tartarin, and said some few words laughingly to his friends.

"Maniloff pretends that we are in the same category with you," explained Sonia to Tartarin. "We also hunt big game!"

" *Tè!* Yes, *pardi* ; wolves, white bears."

" Yes, wolves ; white bears, and other beasts still more detestable ! "

The laughing began again, strident, interminable, in fierce and penetrating tones this time ; laughs which displayed the teeth, and recalled to Tartarin the peculiar character of the company in which he was travelling.

Suddenly the carriages pulled up. The road was becoming stiff, and in this place made a long circuitous bend to reach the top of the Brünig, which could be reached in twenty minutes by a footpath through the beech-wood.  Notwithstanding the morning's rain, and the wet and slippery ground, the tourists, taking advantage of a break in the clouds, nearly all got out, and proceeded in a long file in the narrow path.

From Tartarin's landau, which came last, the men descended; but Sonia, finding the paths very muddy, settled herself in the carriage, and as the Alpinist was following the others, somewhat retarded by his equipment, she said to him in a low tone—and in a very insinuating manner too—" Remain here, and keep me company!" The poor man stood still, quite overwhelmed, weaving for himself a romance as delicious as unlikely, which made his old heart throb loudly and fast.

He was quickly undeceived when he perceived the young lady bending anxiously to watch Bolibine and the Italian at the entrance of the path, behind Maniloff and Boris who were already ahead. The pretended tenor hesitated. Some instinct seemed to warn him not to trust himself alone with these men. He made up his mind at last, and Sonia watched him ascending, caressing her cheek with a bunch of violet cyclamen - those mountain violets, the leaf of which is toned with the fresh colour of the flowers.

The landau proceeded at a slow pace; the coachman was walking with his comrades, and the train of fifteen carriages proceeded upwards silent and empty.

Tartarin felt disturbed by some presentiment of sinister import, not daring to look at his companion, so greatly did he fear that a word or a glance might make him an actor or an accomplice in the drama which he felt was about to take place. But Sonia paid no attention to him: with abstracted eyes she continued to caress the soft down of her cheek, mechanically, with the bunch of flowers.

Then she said after a long pause: "So you know who we are—I and my friends? Well, what do you think of us? What do the French people think of us?"

The hero grew pale and then red. He did not wish to anger, by any imprudent statements, people so vindictive as these; on the other hand, how could he make a compact with assassins? He got out of the difficulty by using a metaphor:

"Well, mademoiselle, you told me just now that we were in the same category, hunters of hydras and monsters, of despots and carnivora. So as a *confrère* of St. Hubert I will reply. My opinion is that even when dealing with wild beasts we ought to meet them with honest weapons. Our Jules Gérard

—the famous lion-hunter—used explosive bullets. I myself do not recognise such things, and I never used them. When I went in pursuit of the lion or the panther, I stood up before the animal face to face with my double-barrelled gun—and—bang! bang!—went a bullet into each eye!"

"In each eye!" said Sonia.

"Never once did I miss my aim!"

He said so: he still believed it himself.

The young lady regarded him with *naïve* admiration, thinking aloud:

"It is a good thing that he should have been quite sure of it."

A quick tearing aside of the branches of the briars, and the thicket opened above them so suddenly, in so feline a manner, that Tartarin, whose head was full of hunting adventures, could have believed he was on the watch in the Zaccar. Maniloff leaped from the thicket noiselessly, close to the carriage. His little wrinkled eyes burned; his face was scratched by the brambles, his beard and his hair were dripping with moisture. Panting for breath, his great hands resting on the carriage-door, he said a few words in Russian to Sonia, who, turning to Tartarin, said sharply:

"Your rope—Quick!"

"My—my rope?"

"Quick, quick! You shall have it again immediately."

Without deigning any other explanation, with her own little gloved hands she assisted him to unfasten the famous rope, made at Avignon. Maniloff took the coil joyfully, and regained the summit of the bank in two bounds, with the activity of a wild cat.

"What is going on? What are they going

to do? He looked very ferocious," muttered Tartarin, not daring to speak his thoughts aloud.

Fierce! Maniloff! Ah, it was easily to be seen that he did not know him. No creature could be better, milder, more compassionate ; and, as instancing this susceptible nature of his, Sonia, with open blue eyes, told him that her friend, after executing the dangerous mandate of the Revolutionary Committee, leaped into the sleigh which awaited him in his flight, and threatened to throw the coachman from his seat if he continued to beat or over-drive the horses on whose speed his own safety depended!

Tartarin thought this trait worthy of the ancients; then, having speculated on all the human lives sacrificed as indiscriminately as an earthquake, or as an active volcano, by Maniloff, who would not have an animal ill-treated, he asked the young lady with an ingenuous air :

"Did he kill many people in the explosion of the Winter Palace?"

"Far too many," Sonia replied sadly.

"And the only one who deserved to die escaped."

She remained silent, as if displeased; and so pretty—the head bent down, and the long, golden lashes resting upon the damask cheek. Tartarin was vexed that he had annoyed her, and captivated by the charms of youthfulness and freshness which seemed to surround this strange little being.

"So, monsieur, the war we wage appears to you unjust and inhuman?" She asked that question with her face close to his, with a caress in her voice and in her eyes: our hero felt himself giving way.

"Do not you think that any means are good and legitimate to deliver a people who are in the death-throes, who are being strangled?"

"No doubt—no doubt."

The young lady, becoming more pressing as Tartarin became weaker, continued:

"You were speaking of a void to be filled, just now; does it not occur to you that it would be more noble, more interesting, to stake your life in a great cause than to risk it in killing lions or in climbing glaciers?"

"The fact is—" said Tartarin, who, quite intoxicated, had lost his head, and was tortured by the mad impulse to seize and kiss that dainty, warm, persuasive hand which she had placed upon his arm, as she had that morning up on the Rigi, when he was putting on her shoe. At length he could control him-

self no longer, and seizing her little gloved hand between his own—

"Listen, Sonia," he cried, in a soft, familiar, and paternal voice; "Listen, Sonia——"

The sudden stoppage of the landau interrupted him. They had reached the summit of the Brünig: tourists and drivers were rejoining their respective carriages, to make up for lost time, and to gain the next village— where *déjeuner* and relays were to be had – at a gallop. The three Russians resumed their places, but that of the Italian remained unoccupied.

"The gentleman has got into one of the first carriages," said Boris to the coachman, who made inquiry concerning him ; and then, addressing himself to Tartarin, whose anxiety was plainly visible, he said:

"We must obtain your rope from him ; he wished to keep it!"

Upon that, fresh bursts of laughter rose in the landau, and caused Tartarin once again the greatest perplexity : he did not know what to think of this good humour and cheerful disposition of the supposed assassins. While wrapping the invalid in plaids and rugs—for the air at that elevation was sharp, and augmented by the pace of the carriage - Sonia related in Russian to her friends the conversation she had had with Tartarin, throwing upon the "bang! bang!" a gentle emphasis which her countrymen repeated after her, some admiring the hero, while Maniloff shook his head incredulously.

The relays!

There is, in the *place* of a large village, an old inn with a worm-eaten wooden balcony, with a rusty hanging iron sign-board. There the file of carriages halted, and while the horses were being changed, the hungry travellers hurried up and crowded into a first-floor room, painted green, which smelt mouldy and damp, where a *table d'hôte* had been laid for twenty people, more or less. There were actually sixty, and for five minutes a regular scramble took place between the Rice and Prune factions round the dishes, to the great alarm of the inn-keeper, who became quite confused, as if the "post" did not pass his door every day at the same time, and he bustled his servants about, who were also seized with a chronic aberration of intellect—

an excellent excuse for only serving half the dishes enumerated on the *carte*, and to give a fantastic change of their own, in which the white *sou* pieces of Switzerland count as half-francs!

"Suppose we breakfast in the carriage?" said Sonia, who was tired; and as nobody had time to attend to them the young people undertook to wait. Maniloff returned brandishing a cold leg of mutton, Bolibine with a long roll and sausages; but the best forager of all was Tartarin. No doubt there was an excellent opportunity for him to leave his companions in the hubbub, and to assure himself concerning the fate of the Italian, but he did not think of that: he was entirely occupied by the prospect of breakfasting with "*la petite*," and of showing Maniloff and the others what a native of Tarascon could do in the way of supplies.

When he descended the steps of the hotel, with a grave and resolute face, holding a tray on which were plates, *serviettes*, and different kinds of food, with Swiss champagne in gold foil, Sonia clapped her hands and complimented him:

"How *did* you manage to get all this?"

"I don't know—one manages it somehow—we are all like that in Tarascon."

Oh! those happy moments. They will be red-letter minutes in the hero's life. That delightful breakfast, seated opposite Sonia, almost on her knees, as in a scene at the opera: the village market-place with its green quincunx, beneath which the silver ornaments and the dresses of the Swiss women glanced brightly as they paced about, two and two like dolls.

How good the bread seemed to be, and what savory sausages! The sky itself was sympathetic, — soft, veiled, but not inclement. There was rain, certainly, but such gentle rain —"lost drops"—just enough to tone down the Swiss champagne, which is dangerous for Southern heads.

Under the veranda of the hotel were four Tyrolese, two giants and two dwarfs, in heavy ragged costumes of staring colours, who, it was said, released by the bankruptcy of a show at a fair, were now mingling their "goose-notes,"—"*aou aou*,"— with the clatter of plates and glasses. They stood there, ugly. stupid, inert, stretching the tendons of their thin necks! Tartarin thought them delightful, and threw them handfuls of coppers, to the great astonishment of the villagers who had assembled round the unhorsed landau.

"*Fife le Vranze!*" exclaimed a tremulous voice from the crowd, out of which pushed his way a tall old man, clothed in a curious blue uniform with silver buttons, the skirts of his coat sweeping the ground behind him. He wore an enormous shako in the shape of a sauerkraut trough, and so heavy with its great plume that the old man was obliged to balance himself with his arms extended as he walked, like a tight-rope dancer.

"*Fieux soltat—carte royale—Charles tix!*"

The Tarasconnais, still mindful of the tales told him by Bompard, began to laugh, and covertly winked.

"I know you, my friend!" But nevertheless he gave him a piece of silver, and poured him out a bumper, which the old man accepted smilingly and with another wink, without knowing why. Then, taking from the side of his mouth an enormous porcelain pipe, he raised his glass and drank "to the company," a circumstance which confirmed

Tartarin in his opinion that the man was a colleague of Bompard.

Never mind: one toast was as good as another!

Then, standing up in the carriage, Tartarin, in a loud voice and with uplifted glass, brought tears to his own eyes, by drinking, first to France, his native land, and afterwards to hospitable Switzerland, which he was happy thus publicly to honour, and to thank, for the generous reception which she bestowed upon all conquered people, and all exiles. Lastly, lowering his voice, the glass inclined towards his travelling companions, he wished them a speedy return to their own land, where he trusted they might find kind relatives and faithful friends, honourable employment, and the termination of all dissensions; for people cannot spend their lives in destroying each other.

While he was enunciating this toast, the brother of Sonia smiled coldly and deprecatingly behind his glasses; Maniloff, with extended neck, his frowning brows making a furrow on his forehead, asked himself if that "*barine*" was never going to stop babbling; while Bolibine, perched on the seat, and screwing up his queer face, which was yellow and wrinkled like a Tartar's, looked like a wretched little monkey perched on the shoulders of Tartarin.

The young lady only listened to him: she was very serious, and endeavouring to understand this curious type of individual. Did he mean all he had said? Had he done all he had related? Is he a fool, or only a braggart, like the deceptive Maniloff, who, in his capacity of a man of action, gave to the word a misleading significance?

The test was about to be applied. His speech concluded, Tartarin was about to resume his seat when a sound of fire-arms was heard—three shots in succession, which at once caused him to rise in some excitement, his ear on the alert; he scented powder.

"Who is firing? where is it? what is happening?"

In his inventive brain quite a little drama was being played—the attack on the convoy by an armed band; an occasion to defend the life and honour of this charming girl.

"Only time enough to load a double-barrelled gun."

But no; the firing came merely from the stand where the young men of the village practised shooting on Sundays. Tartarin airily suggested that they should go so far. He had his idea in proposing this; Sonia had hers in accepting. Guided by the old soldier of the royal guard, still undulating beneath his heavy shako, the party crossed the market-place, dividing the ranks of the crowd, who followed them with some curiosity.

With its thatched roof and newly-cut fir supports, the stand resembled, in a very rustic fashion, one of the (French) shooting-galleries at fairs, at which amateurs practise with old-fashioned, muzzle-loading weapons, which they handle cleverly enough. Silent, with folded arms, Tartarin watched the shooting, criticising it in a loud voice, giving advice—but he did not shoot. The Russians noticed all this, and made signs to each other.

"Bang! bang!" laughed Bolibine, with a gesture of aiming a gun, and imitating the accent of Tarascon: "Pan! pan!"

Tartarin turned round, scarlet, and bursting with rage:

"*Parfaitemain*, young man. Pan! pan!— and as many times as you please."

In the time necessary to load a double-barrelled gun, which had served for generations of chamois-hunters, Tartarin was ready. Pan! pan! He had done it! Both bullets were in the mouth of the figure. A hurrah of admiration rose from all sides. Sonia was triumphant. Bolibine did not laugh.

"That is nothing at all," said Tartarin. "You shall see."

The stand did not suffice; he sought a mark, something to knock over, and the crowd recoiled, dismayed, before this strange Alpinist, with his gun in his hand, who was suggesting to the old guardsman to permit him to knock his pipe from between his teeth at fifty paces. The old man uttered a cry of terror, ran away, and endeavoured to conceal himself in the crowd, over the heads of which his plume nodded continually. Nevertheless Tartarin felt constrained to put the bullet into something. "*Tè, pardi!* like at Tarascon!" And the old sportsman—the *chasseur de casquettes*—threw his head-piece into the air with all the strength of his "double muscles," fired, and put the ball through it. "Bravo!" said Sonia, placing in the little hole, made by the bullet in the cloth, the bouquet with which she had lately been caressing her cheek.

With this beautiful trophy, Tartarin got into the carriage again. The horn was blown, the string of carriages started at a rapid pace down the hill along that marvellous *corniche* road cut in the rocks, where only posts six feet apart protect the traveller from a fall of more than a thousand feet. But Tartarin no longer thought of danger; he no longer gazed upon the landscape. Softened by tender reflections, he admired the pretty child opposite, thinking that glory is only doubtful happiness, that it is a sad thing to grow old alone in so great grandeur, like Moses; and that this cold flower of the North, transplanted into the little garden at Tarascon, would dissipate the monotony of the everlasting baobab (*Arbos gigantea*) in its tiny pot. Sonia gazed at him also, and thought—but who can ever tell of what young ladies think!

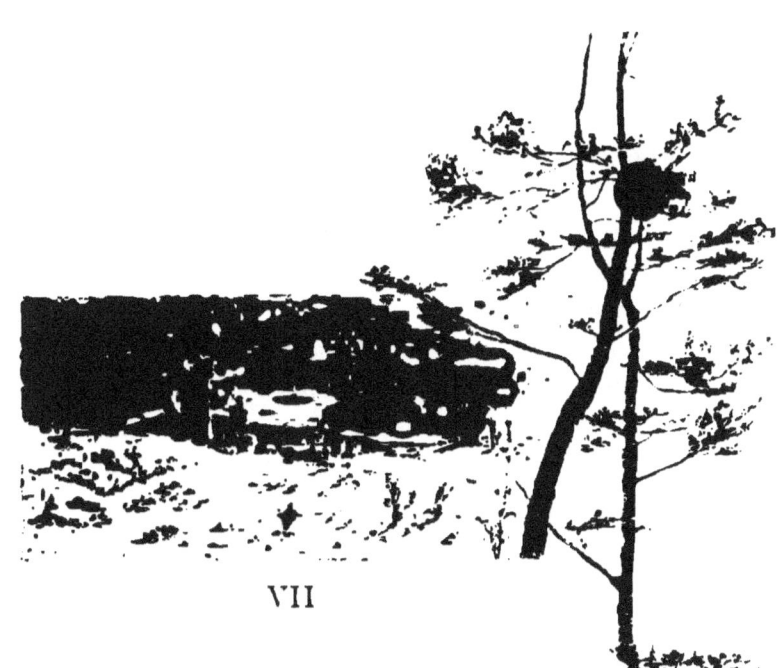

VII

*Night at Tarascon.—Where is he? — Anxiety
— The "cigales du Cours" demand Tartarin.
— Martyrdom of a Tarascon saint. — The
Alpine Club. — What happened at the
chemist's.—Help! Bézuquet.*

"A LETTER, M. Bézuquet. It comes from Switzerland, vé! —from Switzerland," exclaimed the postman joyfully across the little court, as he waved something in the air, and hurried up as the summer evening was closing in.

The chemist, who was enjoying the fresh air in his shirt-sleeves at his door, bounded forward, seized the letter with trembling hands, and carried it into his "den," which was redolent of various elixirs and dried herbs, but he did not open the missive until the postman had gone, refreshed by a glass of the delicious *Sirop de Cadavre* as a reward for his good news.

For fifteen days had Bézuquet been expecting this letter from Switzerland—fifteen days of agonising suspense! Now here it is! And while only looking at the small and determined address on the envelope, the post-mark of Interlachen and the large violet stamp of the "Hôtel Jungfrau, kept by Meyer," tears filled his eyes, and caused those heavy Barbary-corsair moustaches to tremble with emotion.

"*Confidential: destroy when read.*"

These words in large letters at the head of the page, and in the telegrammic style of the Pharmacopœia—"For external use only: to be well shaken before being applied,"—troubled the recipient so greatly that he read them aloud as one speaks in bad dreams.

"What has happened to me is appalling!"

In the next room, Madame Bézuquet, his

mother, who was in the habit of taking a little nap, after supper, could hear him as well as the pupil who kept braying something in a great mortar in the laboratory. Bézuquet continued his reading in a low voice—began again two or three times, very pale, while his hair literally stood up on his head! Then, with a rapid glance around him—*cra cra*—there was the letter in a thousand little bits tossed into the waste-paper basket: but it could be pieced together again, perhaps! While he was stooping to pick them up, a querulous voice cried:

"*Vé*, Ferdinand, are you there?"

"Yes, *maman*," replied the unhappy corsair, congealed with fear, all his great body under the desk as he groped for the pieces of the letter.

"What are you doing, my treasure?"

"I am,—*hé*—I am making—the eye-salve for Mademoiselle Tournatoire."

The mother went to sleep again; the pestle of the pupil, suspended for the moment, again resumed the monotonous movement which lulled to sleep the household, already

exhausted by the fatigue of the hot summer day.
Bézuquet now paced up and down before his
door, by turns red or green according as he

passed one or other of his bottles. He
gesticulated, jerking out words at intervals:
" Poor fellow! lost! fatal attachment; how can
he be extracted from this?"—and notwithstanding his anxiety he accompanied with a
lively whistle the " retreat " played by the dra-
goons under the plane-trees of the *Tour de ville*.

"*Hé!* adieu, Bézuquet," said a shadow, hurrying through the grey twilight.

"Where are you off to, Pégoulade?"

"To the club; there is a meeting to-night. We are to discuss Tartarin and the presidency. We must attend."

"*Tè*, yes! I will come," replied the chemist, suddenly. He had conceived a providential idea. He went inside, put on his overcoat, and searched his pockets to assure himself that his latch key and the American knuckle-duster, without which no native of Tarascon would venture out after "retreat," were safe. Then he called for Pascalon, but in subdued tones, for fear of arousing the old lady.

Almost a youth, and already bald, as if he wore all his hair in his frizzly fair beard, the pupil Pascalon had the elevated soul of a fanatic, a forehead like a dome, eyes like an idiotic gnat, and on his cheeks pimples of various delicate tones, crusty and golden, like a little loaf of Beaucaire. On great days and festivals the club intrusted its banner to this youth who had vowed to the P. C. A. a fierce admiration, the silent, but burning, devotion of the candle which consumes itself upon the altar at Easter-tide.

"Pascalon," whispered the chemist, so close to his pupil's head that the tip of his moustache entered his ear, "I have had news of Tartarin! It is harrowing!"

Then, seeing his assistant grow paler, he continued:

"Courage, my lad, all may yet be repaired. *Différemment* to you I confide the shop. If any one asks for arsenic, don't let him have it; if any one asks for opium, don't give it to him; nor rhubarb either— nor anything! If I am not back at ten o'clock, shut up and go to bed. Go!"

With intrepid steps he plunged into the darkness of the *Tour de ville* without once looking behind him, a circumstance which gave Pascalon the opportunity to rush to the waste-paper basket, and to search with eager and trembling hands, to turn the contents out at last upon the desk, in his anxiety to ascertain whether some bits of the mysterious letter did not remain.

Any one who knows the exaltation of the Tarasconnais will readily understand the state of excitement the little town had been in since the sudden disappearance of Tartarin. And besides, *pas moins, différemment*, they had all lost their heads, all the more because they were now in the middle of August, and their craniums were broiling under a sun hot enough to boil their kettles. From morning till night nothing was heard in the town but the name of "Tartarin," whether on the pinched lips of the old women with hoods, or in the cherry mouths of the *grisettes* with velvet ribbons in their hair: "Tartarin, Tartarin," and, under the plane-trees of the *Cours*, laden with white dust, the hidden grasshoppers seemed to give vent to the two sounding syllables, "Tar--tar—tar—tar--tar."

As no one knew anything whatever about him, it was only natural that every one should be well informed, and be able to give an ex-

planation of the departure of the President. There were the most extravagant versions. According to some, he had become a Trappist, he had carried away the Dugazon; others said that he had emigrated to found a colony which would be called Port Tarascon, or even that he had penetrated into Central Africa in search of Doctor Livingstone!

"Ah! vaï, Livingstone! Why he died two years ago!"

But the Tarascon imagination defies all considerations of time and space. And the curious part of the matter was that all these

tales of La Trappe, colonisation, distant voyages, &c., were ideas of Tartarin himself; visions of that waking dreamer, already communicated to his intimate friends, who did not know what to think; and felt very much annoyed in their secret hearts at not being told; while affecting with others an ostentatious reserve, a knowing and crafty air!

Excourbaniès suspected Bravida of knowing all about it, and Bravida on his part said: " Bézuquet must be acquainted with all this. He looks askance like a dog carrying a bone!"

It is a fact that the chemist suffered a thousand deaths with this secret like a hair-shirt, smarting and itching ; making him grow pale and red in the same minute, and causing him to squint continually. Just think that the poor wretch was in Tarascon, and say whether, in all the *Book of Martyrs*, there is to be found a torture so terrible as his the martyrdom of Saint Bézuquet, who knew something and was not permitted to divulge it!

This is the reason why that evening, notwithstanding the terrible news, his step was so light, so free, almost running as he went to the meeting. *Enfin!* He was going to speak : to unbosom himself, to tell what had so long weighed on his mind, and in his haste to free himself he threw out interjectional remarks at the passers-by in the *Tour de ville*. The day had been so hot that notwithstanding the unwonted hour and the terrifying darkness— it was a quarter to eight by the town clock—

there was out of doors a merry crowd, tradesmen's families seated on the benches and enjoying the fresh air while their houses were cooling; bands of factory-girls walked five or six abreast, holding each other's arms, in an undulating, chattering, laughing line. In all these groups they were speaking of Tartarin.

"Well, Monsieur Bézuquet, no letter yet?" asked one, stopping the chemist in his walk.

"Yes, indeed, my friend; I beg your pardon! Read the *Forum* to-morrow morning."

He hurried on, but they followed him, pressed upon him, and there ran a murmur along the drive, a trampling of feet, that halted under the windows of the club, which were open, throwing large square patches of light upon the ground.

The meeting was being held in the old card-room, in which the long table covered with green cloth served as a desk. In the centre of it was the President's chair with P. C. A. embroidered on the back; and the chair of the secretary faced it. Behind was displayed the banner, above a long map *in relievo* of the *Alpines*, with their respective names and altitudes. Alpenstocks of honour, mounted in ivory in racks like billiard-cues, embellished the corners, and

the glass cases displayed curiosities picked up on the mountains—crystals, flints, petrifactions, two sea-urchins, and a salamander!

In the absence of Tartarin, Costecalde, looking radiant, rejuvenated, occupied the

"It is false! The President *has* written!"

chair. The secretary's seat was filled by Excourbaniès; but this devil of a fellow, frizzled, shaggy, and bearded, felt the need of noise or of agitation, which did not fit him for performing secretarial duties. On the smallest pretext he would throw up his arms and legs, utter the most alarming cries, and shout "Ha! ha! ha!" in his ferocious joy, which generally terminated in the terrible war-cry of the residents of Tarascon in their idiom —"*Fen dé brut!*—let us make a noise!" They called him "The Gong," because his brazen tones were continually dinning in one's ears.

Here and there about the room the other members of the Committee were seated.

In the first line was the former *capitaine d'habillement*, Bravida, whom every one in Tarascon called the Commandant—a very small man, as neat as a new pin, who compensated himself for his small stature by cultivating the wild and moustached head and face of Vercingetorix.

Then we perceive the long, seamed, and sickly face of Pégoulade, the tax-collector, the sole survivor of the wreck of the *Medusa*. Always, as far as the memory of man extended, there had been in Tarascon a sole survivor of the wreck of the *Medusa*. At one time, indeed, there had been three, who mutually looked upon each other as impostors, and would not associate with each other. Of the three, the true one was Pégoulade. Shipped on board the *Medusa* with his parents, he had experienced the disaster when he was six months old, but this circumstance did not prevent him from recounting, as *an eye-witness*, the minutest details of the famine, the boats, the raft, and he told how he had seized by the neck the captain, who had endeavoured to save himself —"the wretch!" At six months old! *Outre!* Always boring people with his everlasting story, which everybody knew before, filtered through fifty years, and which gave him a pretext for giving himself an injured, desolate air, apart from life, as it were. "After what I have seen," he would say, and very unjustly, since he had retained his position as tax-gatherer through every administration.

Near him were the brothers Rognonas, twins and sexagenarians, never deserting each other, but always quarrelling and making rude remarks to each other. There was so great a resemblance between their two old, worn, and irregularly-shaped heads, that, had they been placed facing in opposite directions for antipathy, they might have figured in a medallion with IANVS BIFRONS as a legend.

In other chairs were scattered President Bédaride, Barjavel the advocate, Cambalalette the notary, and the terrible Doctor Tournatoire, who, Bravida said, "would let blood from a turnip!"

The heat was increasing, being much augmented by the gas, so these gentlemen sat in their shirt-sleeves, a circumstance which rather detracted from the dignity of the meeting. It is true they were in private, and the infamous Costecalde wished to profit by it to advance the date of the election, without waiting for the return of Tartarin. Assured of success, he triumphed in advance, and when, after the reading of the orders of the day by Excourbaniès, he rose to work his plot out, a horrible smile curved his thin lips.

"Beware of him who smiles before speaking," muttered the Commandant.

Costecalde, without flinching, and with a wink to the faithful Tournatoire, began in a thin voice:

"Gentlemen, the indefensible conduct of our President,— the uncertainty in which he leaves us——"

"It is false! The President has written!"

Bézuquet, trembling, planted himself before the table; but remembering that his attitude was "unparliamentary," he changed his tone, and with uplifted hand, according to custom, requested leave to make a statement on a pressing question.

"Speak! Speak!"

Costecalde, very yellow, and with throat compressed, gave him permission with a nod. Then, and not till then, Bézuquet began:

"Tartarin is at the foot of the Jungfrau. He is about to ascend it. He requests that the banner may be sent to him."

A silence, broken only by the hard breathing of the audience and the burning of the gas, succeeded. Then a loud hurrah, an uproar of "bravos" and stamping, which overbore the gong of Excourbaniès, who uttered his war-whoop, "Ha! ha! ha! *fen dé brut!*" to which the anxious crowd without responded with cheers.

Costecalde, becoming more and more yellow, rang the presidential bell desperately. At length Bézuquet continued, mopping his forehead and puffing as if he was ascending five stories high.

Now, about this banner, which their President demanded, with a view to planting it on the virgin summit, were they going to tie it up, and send it, packed like an ordinary case, by express?

"Never! Ha! ha! ha!" roared Excourbaniès.

Would it not be better to appoint a delegation by lot?

They would not permit him to finish. While you could say "*Zou!*" the proposition was carried by acclamation, the names of the three delegates were chosen in the following order: (1) Bravida, (2) Pégoulade, (3) the chemist.

No. 2 protested. The lengthy journey alarmed him, so weak and ill had he been since the accident to the *Medusa*.

"I will go in your place, Pégoulade," roared Excourbaniès, making a semaphore of his limbs. As for Bézuquet, he could not leave his pharmacy. It was necessary for the safety of the town that he should remain. One indiscreet act on the part of the pupil, and Tarascon would be poisoned, decimated!

"*Outre!*" said the Committee, rising as one man.

180   *Tartarin on the Alps*

It was certain that the chemist could not go, because he could not leave Pascalon alone, but he could send Pascalon, who would carry the banner. That he would

know how to do. On this, more acclamations, a fresh burst of clangour from the Gong, and outside another popular demonstration, so great that Excourbaniès felt constrained to show himself at the window, and his unrivalled voice was soon heard above the tumult.

"My friends, Tartarin is found. He is in a fair way to cover himself with glory."

Without adding more than "*Vive Tartarin,*"

his war-whoop was uttered with all the force of his lungs; it dominated the terrible clamour of the great crowd under the trees of the *Cours*, rolling on and echoing in the cloud of dust until it reached the trees whereon it compelled the trembling grasshoppers to pipe up again as if in mid-day!

Hearing that, Costecalde, who had approached a window, as well as all the others, returned to his chair with unsteady steps.

"*Vé*, Costecalde," said some one, "what is the matter? How yellow he is!"

Every one ran away then, for the terrible Tournatoire was bringing out his lancet, but the gun-maker, writhing in apparent pain, murmured, through a hideous grimace, ingenuously:

"Nothing—it is nothing. Leave me—it is the envy!"

Poor Costecalde, he had indeed all the appearance of suffering!

While these events were taking place, at the other side of the *Tour de ville*, in the chemist's shop, Bézuquet's pupil, seated on his patron's counter, was patiently collecting and putting together bit by bit the fragments left by the chemist in the waste-paper basket; but numerous pieces could not be re-united. Here was the strange and startling puzzle put before him, very like a map of Central Africa, with spaces—the blanks of *terra incognita*, which the terrified imagination of the simple banner-bearer was exploring:

<pre>
                        mad for love
       lamp à chalum   Chicago preserves
can scarce tear mys   Nihilist
to death   condition abom   in exchange
of her   You know me, Ferdi
                        know my liberal notions,
but from that to Czaricide
                rrible consequences
Siberia   hung   adore her
            Ah !   shake thy faithful han
                        Tar   Tar
</pre>

VIII

Memorable dialogue between the Jungfrau and Tartarin. — A Nihilist salon. — The duel with hunting-knives. — Horrible nightmare. — "'Tis I whom you seek, gentlemen?" — Strange reception of the Tarascon delegates at the Hôtel Meyer.

LIKE all the fashionable hotels in Interlachen, the Hôtel Jungfrau, kept by Meyer, is situated on the Hœheweg, a wide promenade between rows of chestnut-trees which vaguely recalled to Tartarin his beloved *Tour de ville* without the sun, the dust, and the grasshoppers, for the rain had not ceased for a week.

He had a capital room, with a balcony, on the first floor; and in the morning, when trimming his beard before a little hand-glass — an old habit of his — the first object that met his gaze, beyond the corn, and the lavender, and the firs, in a frame of dark green, rising by successive stages, was the Jungfrau, its peak-like summit emerging from the clouds, a pure white mass of snow, upon which the rays of an invisible sunrise rested daily. Then, between the red and white Alp and the Alpinist of Tarascon arose a short dialogue which was not wanting in grandeur.

"Tartarin, are we ready?" inquired the Jungfrau severely.

"*Voilà*, I am ready," replied the hero, his thumb beneath his nose, hastening to finish his beard; and very quickly he dressed as far as his check suit, which had not been worn for some days. He passed it by, grumbling:

"*Coquin de sort!* it is true that is no word — "

But a clear and pleasant voice now arose

amid the myrtles which lined the windows of the *rez-de-chaussée:*

"Good morning," said Sonia, seeing him appear upon the balcony; "the landau is waiting for us—make haste, you lazy man!"

"I am coming; I am coming!"

In "two twos" he had substituted a linen shirt for his flannel one; for his knickerbockers a serpent-green suit with which he had been in the habit of turning the heads of all the Tarascon ladies on Sundays.

The landau was waiting in front of the hotel. Sonia was already seated beside her brother, who was growing paler and paler day by day, notwithstanding the healthy air of Interlachen; but at the moment of departure Tartarin saw approaching, with all the deliberation of bears, two famous guides of Grindelwald, Rudolf Kaufmann and Christian Inebnit, engaged by him for the ascent of the Jungfrau, and who every morning came to see whether their employer was disposed to attempt it.

The appearance of these two men, wearing strong hobnailed boots, fustian jackets, rubbed on the shoulder by the knapsack and rope, their simple and serious faces, the four words of French which they stumbled over as they twirled their great hats in their hands, was

veritable torture for Tartarin. He had better have said:

"Don't disturb yourselves; I will come to you first."

Every day he found them in the same place, and got rid of them by a "tip" in proportion to the magnitude of his remorse. Very much delighted to do the Jungfrau in such pleasant fashion, the guides pocketed the *trinkgeld* gravely, and with resigned steps returned to their village in the fine rain, leaving Tartarin confused and desperate in his weakness. But the beautiful air, the flowery plains, reflected in the clear pupils of Sonia's bright eyes, the touch of her little foot on his boot in the carriage——To the devil with the Jungfrau! The hero only thought of his love, or rather of the mission which had been assigned to him to turn into the right way this poor little Sonia—an unconscious criminal, cast, in consequence of her devotion to her brother, beyond the pale of the law and of nature.

This was the motive which kept him in Interlachen, in the same hotel as the Wassiliefs. At his age, with his fatherly air, he could not— it was out of the question that he should—fall in love with this child; only he perceived she was so gentle, so kind, so generous towards all the miserable people of her party, so devoted to her brother, who had returned from the Siberian mines covered with ulcers, poisoned with verdigris, condemned to death

by consumption more surely than by any
number of courts-martial! There was something
to touch him in all this, *allons!*

Tartarin suggested that they should come
to Tarascon, and he would accommodate
them in a cottage full of sunlight at the gates
of the town, that charming little town where
it never rains, where life passes in singing and
fêtes. He got excited, pretended to play a
tambourine on his hat, and hummed the gay
national air to a *farandole:*

> *Lagadigadèu
> La Tarasco, La Tarasco,
> Lagadigadèu
> La Tarasco de Casteù.*

But while an ironical smile thinned the lips
of the invalid, Sonia shook her head. No
fêtes, no sun for her, so long as the Russian
people groaned beneath the tyrant. So soon
as her brother had recovered — his sunken
eyes told another tale — nothing would prevent
her from returning to Russia to suffer and to
die for the sacred cause.

"But, *coquin de bon sort!*" exclaimed Tartarin, "after this present tyrant has been blown up, there will be another! You will then have to begin all over again! And so time passes—*vé!* the time for happiness and love." His manner of pronouncing *amour*, in the Tarascon dialect, with three *r*'s, and his eyes starting out of his head, amused the young girl: but then, seriously, she could never love any man but one who would save her native land. Yes, were he as ugly as Bolibine, more rustic and rough-looking than Maniloff, she was prepared to give herself up to him, to live with him *en libre grâce*, so long as her youth lasted, or until he was tired of her!

"*En libre grâce!*" is the term used by the Nihilists to describe the unions illegally contracted between them by mutual consent. And of this primitive style of marriage Sonia spoke calmly, with her maiden face opposite Tartarin, a good citizen, a peaceable elector, —but quite disposed, nevertheless, to end his days with this adorable girl in the said state of "free grace" if she had not saddled it with so many murders, and such-like horrible conditions.

While they were discussing these exceedingly delicate topics, the fields, the lakes, the woods, the mountains were being unfolded

before them, and ever, at every turning, through every shower of the perpetual wet days which followed the hero in his excursions, the Jungfrau uplifted her white peak as if to sharpen the edge of his remorse for that beautiful excursion. The party returned to *déjeuner*, and seated themselves at the long table, where the Rice and Prune factions preserved their hostile attitude, and silent as ever; but Tartarin was perfectly unconcerned about them, as he sat beside Sonia, watching to see that Boris did not have a window open behind him, solicitous, attentive, paternal,

airing all his seductions as a man of the world, and his domestic qualities as an excellent domestic rabbit!

Afterwards they took tea in the Russian apartments, in the little *salon* on the ground floor at the end of the garden, by the side of the promenade. Another charming hour of intimate conversation in a low tone for Tartarin, while Boris slept on a sofa. The hot water bubbled in the *samovar*, a smell of watered flowers came in through the half-open door, with the blue tint of the glass frame. A little more sun and heat, and it would have been the realisation of Tartarin's dream—his little Russian seated by him, tending the small garden in which the baobab grew!

Suddenly Sonia jumped up:

"Two o'clock! And the letters?"

"Here goes," cried the worthy Tartarin, and by nothing but his accent, the manner in which he buttoned up his coat, and balanced his cane, could you have guessed the gravity of his errand, so simple in appearance, viz., to go to the post-office to find the Wassiliefs' letters.

Very closely watched by the local authorities and the Russian police, the Nihilists, particularly the chiefs, were compelled to take certain precautions, such as having their letters addressed to the *poste restante*, and with initials only.

Since their arrival at Interlachen, Boris had

scarcely been able to get about. Tartarin, with a view to spare Sonia the long wait at the *guichet*, under the gaze of many eyes, was charged with the risks and perils of the correspondence. The post-office is only ten minutes' walk from the hotel, in the wide street which is a continuation of the promenade, and bordered with *cafés*, beer-shops, shops for tourists' alpenstocks, gaiters, straps, opera-glasses, tinted spectacles, flasks, travelling-bags, everything that would serve to make a renegade climber ashamed of himself. Tourists passed in caravans—horses, guides, mules, blue veils, green veils, with the rattling of canteens, and the ambling of animals, the iron tips of sticks marking the steps; but this *fête*, ever renewed, left Tartarin indifferent. He did not even feel the *bise* and the puffs of snow which came down from the mountains, being only attentive to throw off the scent the spies whom he believed were on his track.

The first soldier of the advance-guard, the first skirmisher skirting the wall of an enemy's town, does not advance with more circumspection than did our hero during his short excursion from the hotel to the post office. At the least sound of footsteps behind him, he stopped attentively at the photographic shops,

or turned a few pages of an English or German book, in order to compel the detective to pass him; or sometimes he would turn suddenly round, to perceive, with his fierce eyes, a girl from one of the inns carrying or going for provisions; or some inoffensive tourist, an old Prune from the *table d'hôte*, who would step off the pavement astonished, taking him for an idiot.

When he reached the "*poste*," the pigeonhole of which opens right upon the street, Tartarin passed and repassed before he approached; then suddenly he hastened forward, pushed his head and shoulders into the

"Watched the faces before he approached."

aperture, muttering some indistinct words, which they always asked him to repeat, a course which made him savage, and at length, having received his letters, he regained the hotel by a long *détour* by the kitchens, his hand clenched in his pocket upon the packet of letters and papers, ready to tear them up and swallow them on the least alarm.

Maniloff and Bolibine nearly always waited for the news in their friends' apartments. From motives of prudence and economy they did not lodge in the hotel. Bolibine had found work in a printing-office, and Maniloff, a very skilful cabinet-maker, worked for contractors. The Tarasconnais did not love these men; the one bored him with his grimaces and his bantering manner, the other haunted him with his fierce airs. Besides, they occupied too much of Sonia's heart.

"He is a hero," she had said to him when talking of Bolibine, and she related how, during three years, he had, unaided, printed a revolutionary paper in St. Petersburg. Three years he did this, without coming down stairs once, and without showing himself at a window, sleeping in a large cupboard, where the woman with whom he lodged concealed him every evening with his clandestine printing-machine.

And, again, the life of Maniloff during six months in the underground cellars of the Winter Palace, biding his time, sleeping every night upon his store of dynamite, which gave him intolerable headaches, and nervous attacks, still more enhanced by the ceaseless anguish, the sudden appearances of the police vaguely conscious that a mine was being prepared, and coming suddenly to surprise the workmen employed in the Palace. At his rare exits, Maniloff would be accosted on the Admiralty Square by a delegate of the Revolutionary Committee, who demanded, in a whisper :

" Is it done ? "

" No, nothing yet," the other would reply, without moving his lips. At length, cne evening in February, the same question was put in the same terms ; he replied with the greatest coolness :

" It is done."

Almost immediately afterwards a bewildering uproar confirmed his words, and all the lights in the Palace were suddenly extinguished, the square was plunged in the deepest obscurity, which was pierced only by the cries of pain and terror, the sounding of trumpets, the galloping of

orderlies, and of the fire-brigade hurrying up with their engines. . . .

Sonia paused in her recital:

"Is this horrible, so many human lives sacrificed? is so much effort, courage, and intelligence useless? No, no; yet, these butcheries *en masse* are bad. The man they aim at always escapes. The true way to proceed, the most humane, would be to go to the Czar as you would approach a lion, determined, well armed, post yourself at a window, or at the door of his carriage, and when he passes ——"

"*Bé oui!* certainly," said Tartarin, who felt much embarrassed, feigning not to understand the allusion; and suddenly he launched into some discussion, philosophic or humanitarian,

with some of the others present. For Bolibine and Maniloff were not the only visitors to the Wassiliefs. Every day some new faces came in, young people, men or women dressed as poor students or fanatical teachers, blonde and rosy, with the obstinate foreheads and the fierce childishness of Sonia, law-breakers, exiles, some of them even under sentence of death, which could in no way detract from their youthful expansiveness.

They laughed, chatting loudly too, and as

the greater number spoke French, Tartarin quickly found himself at his ease. They called him "uncle," divining in him something infantine, *naïf*, which pleased them. Perhaps he rather carried his recitals of his exploits a little too far, baring his arm above the elbow to show where the panther had wounded him, or displaying beneath his beard the holes which the claws of the lion of the Atlas had made ; perhaps, also, he became familiar with his friends too soon, putting his arm round them, slapping them on the shoulders, calling them by their Christian names in about five minutes after being introduced, as thus :

"Listen, Dmitri," "You know me, Fedor Ivanovitch," or at any rate within a very short time; but he "went down" with them all the same, by his plain-dealing, his amiability, his confident air, and by his desire to please. They read their letters in his presence, discussed their plans and passwords to blindfold the police—a purely conspirators' view which tickled Tartarin's imagination very much ; and although he was by nature opposed to acts of violence, he could not at times help discussing their homicidal projects, approving, criticising, offering advice dictated by the experience of a great chief who has been upon the war-path, accustomed to the management of all kinds of weapons, and to personal encounters with wild beasts.

One day, when they were talking in his presence of the assassination of a police officer by a Nihilist at the theatre, he demonstrated to them that the thrust had been badly given, and then he gave them a lesson on the use of the knife :

" Like this, *vé!* from below upwards. Thus you do not run any risk of wounding yourself."

Then, exciting himself to his acting level, he said :

"Suppose, *té!* that I have your despot *entre quartre-z'yeux* at a bear-hunt. He is where you are, Fedor ; I am here near the round table, and each has a hunting-knife. We two, *monseigneur*, we must have a turn ! "

Planted in the middle of the room, bending his short legs ready for a spring, stripped like a woodcutter, he imitated for them a real combat, terminating with his cry of triumph when he had plunged his weapon to the hilt upwards, *coquin de sort!* in the entrails of his adversary!

"That is how it is done, young people," he said.

But what retribution, what terrors, he endured when he was no longer under the influence of Sonia's blue eyes, after the mental intoxication which had produced this bouquet of follies, he found himself alone, in his nightcap, face to face with his reflections and his usual nightly glass of *eau sucrée*.

After all, in what was he meddling? The Czar was not his Czar; and all these tales scarcely concerned him. Suppose that, one of these days, he was imprisoned, banished, delivered up to Muscovite justice!

Boufre! all these Cossacks did not joke about that! And in the darkness of his own room, with that horrible faculty of imagina-

tion that the horizontal position increases, now was opened out before him, like one of those sets of unfolding pictures which he used to have given him when a child, the varied and terrible punishments to which he was rendering himself liable; Tartarin in the copper-mines, as Boris had been, working in water up to his waist, his body being slowly eaten away—poisoned. He escapes! hides himself in the midst of snowy forests, pursued by Tartars and dogs trained to hunt fugitives. Worn out by cold and hunger, he is recaptured, and finally hanged between two convicts, embraced by a priest with shiny hair, smelling strongly of brandy and seal-oil, while far away yonder at Tarascon, in the sunlight, sound the *fanfares* of trumpets on a fine Sunday: the crowd —the ungrateful and oblivious populace—are installing the triumphant Costecalde in the chair of the P. C. A.!

It was in the agony of one of these terrible dreams that he shouted, "*A moi, Bézuquet!*" He sent to the chemist that confidential letter under the influence of that horrible nightmare. But the gentle "Good morning" of Sonia again bewitched him, and threw him once again into all the weakness of indecision.

One evening, when returning from the Kursaal to the hotel with the Wassiliefs and Bolibine, after two hours of enthralling music, the miserable man forgot all prudence, and the words "Sonia, I love you!" which he had so long restrained, he at length pronounced, grasping the little arm which rested on his own. She made no sign of emotion, but looked at him fixedly, very pale, under the gas-light where they had stopped: "Well then, deserve me," she said, with a charming but puzzling smile, which displayed all her beautiful teeth. Tartarin was about to reply, binding himself, by an oath, to perform any, deadly deed, when the *chasseur* of the hotel came up and said:

"There are some people for you, up stairs, — some gentlemen. They are looking for you!"

"Looking for me! *Outre!* What for?" Then Number 1 of his dioramic views came before his mind's eye: Tartarin imprisoned— exiled! Certainly he was afraid, but his attitude was heroic. Separating himself quickly from Sonia, he said in a choking voice, "Fly! save yourself!" Then he ascended the stairs, with head erect, and proud mien, as if he were going to execution; but so nervous, nevertheless, that he was obliged to grasp the banisters for support.

When he gained the corridor, he perceived a group of men at the door of his apartment, looking through the keyhole, knocking, and calling to him.

He advanced two paces, and then with parched lips managed to say, "Do you want me, gentlemen?"

"*Té, pardi!* yes, my President!"

A little elderly man, brisk and bony, dressed in a grey suit, and who seemed to be carrying on his coat, his hat, his gaiters, his long pendent moustaches, all the dust of the *Tour de ville*, fell upon the neck of our hero, rubbing against his soft and chubby cheeks the tough hide of the old captain.

"Bravida! it is impossible! Excourbaniès, too!—and who is that yonder?"

A bleating voice replied, "Dear ma-as-ter!" Then the pupil advanced, knocking against the wall as he came a species of long fishing-rod, thick at the top, and swathed in silver paper and oil-cloth.

"*Hé! vé*, it is Pascalon. Let us embrace, *petitot!* But what are you carrying? Put it down!"

"The paper—undo the paper," puffed the Commandant. The youth unrolled it quickly, and the Tarascon banner was displayed to the eyes of the astonished Tartarin.

The delegates took off their hats.

"My President"—Bravida's voice was

trembling, solemn, and husky—"you demanded the banner; we have brought it to you--*té!*"

The President opened his eyes until they became as large as apples:

"I! *I* asked for it?"

"What! didn't you ask for it?"

"Ah! yes, *parfaitemain*," replied Tartarin,

suddenly enlightened by the name of Bézuquet.[1]

Now he understood it all, and guessed what had happened; and feeling overcome by the ingenious deception which Bézuquet had practised with a view to recall him to his duty and to honour, he choked, and muttered in his beard: "Ah, my children, this is kind — what good you do me!"

"*Vive le Présidain!*" squeaked Pascalon, brandishing his "oriflamme." The Gong sounded loudly, and shouted his war-whoop, "Ha! ha! ha! *fen dé brut!*" which penetrated to the cellars of the hotel. Doors were opened, curious faces appeared on every floor. These disappeared quickly at the sight of the standard and of the dark and shaggy men who hurled out strange defiances with extended arms. Never had such a row been heard in the peaceful Jungfrau hotel before.

"Come into my room," said Tartarin, somewhat ashamed. They were feeling their way in the darkness, seeking the match-box,

---

[1] Bézuquet is not mentioned. — *Trans*

when an authoritative rap at the door caused it to open and disclose the arrogant, yellow, puffed visage of Meyer, the hotel proprietor. He was about to enter the room, but stopped in the darkness, in which his fiery eyes gleamed, on the sill, his teeth clenched on his hard Teutonic accents:

"Mind you keep quiet, or I will have you all taken up by the police."

A bellow as from a buffalo followed this discourteous speech, and the brutal use of the word "*ramasser*." The landlord retreated a pace, but flung another sentence into the room:

"We know who you are! Be off! We have our eyes upon you; and I do not want any more people like you in the house!"

"Monsieur Meyer," replied Tartarin calmly, politely, but very firmly, "get my bill made out; these gentlemen and I will leave for the Jungfrau to-morrow morning."

O, native land, O, little country in the

great one, what influence is thine! It was sufficient to hear the Tarascon dialect rustling, with the country air, the blue folds of the banner—when, lo! there is Tartarin delivered from his love, and from the snares which surrounded him, restored to his friends, his mission, and to glory!

Now, *zou!*

IX

At the sign of " The Faithful Chamois."

NEXT day it was delightful to take the footpath from Interlachen to Grindelwald, which the tourists were obliged to pass to pick up the guides for the Little Scheideck ; delightful, the triumphal march of the P. C. A., once more equipped in his mountaineering habiliments, supported on one side by the thin shoulder of the Commandant Bravida, on the other by the robust arm of Excourbaniès, both proud to escort him, to sustain their dear President, to carry his ice-axe, his sac, his alpenstock; while sometimes in front, and sometimes behind, or on the flank, Pascalon gamboled like a little dog, carrying his banner, wisely packed up, so as to avoid any demonstration such as they had had the evening before.

The high spirits of his companions, the sentiment of duty done, the snowy Jungfrau yonder, were not sufficient to make the hero forget what he had left behind him, perhaps for ever, and without a farewell! As he passed the last houses of Interlachen, his eyes filled with tears, and while he was walking he unbosomed himself, turn about, to Excourbaniès with "Listen, Spiridion," or to Bravida with "You know me, Placide"—for, by the irony of fate, the invincible soldier was called Placide, and the rough "buffalo," with material instincts, Spiridion.

Unfortunately, the Tarascon race, more brave than sentimental, never could take love affairs seriously. "Whoever loses a woman and fifteen pence, is to be condoled with for the loss of the money," replied the sententious Placide, and Spiridion quite agreed with him. As for the innocent Pascalon, he held women in fear, and blushed to the eyes when they pronounced the name of *la Petite Scheideck* in his hearing, having a kind of notion that it referred to a lady of somewhat free-and-easy manners. The poor lover was, therefore, obliged to keep his thoughts to himself, and to console himself alone, which is, after all, the safest course.

Besides, what worries could resist the attractions of the route across the narrow, deep, and shaded valley, where the tourists skirted a winding river, white with foam, and roaring like thunder amid the echoing pines which overhung and surrounded it on both its sloping sides!

The Tarasconnais delegates, with their heads held high, advanced with a feeling akin to terror in "religious" admiration; like the companions of Sindbad the Sailor, when they saw the mangroves and other gigantic flora of the Indian coasts. Only hitherto acquainted with their little bare and stony hills, they had no idea that there could possibly grow so many trees at once, on such very high mountains too!

"Oh, that is nothing; wait until you see the

Jungfrau," remarked the P. C. A., who quite enjoyed their surprise, and felt himself growing bigger in their estimation.

At the same time, to enliven the scene and to humanise its imposing strain, many parties of people passed them *en route*—large landaus at full trot, with veils floating from the doors—heads were bent in curiosity to see the President surrounded by the delegation; while from time to time wood-carvers' stalls were passed; little girls standing by the wayside, looking very wooden-y in their straw hats with wide ribbons, and party-coloured skirts, singing in chorus of three voices, and offering bouquets of raspberry-sprays and *edelweiss*. Sometimes the Alpine horn would echo through the mountains its melancholy notes, swelling up, and repeated by the gorges, then slowly dying away after the manner of a cloud resolving into vapour.

"It is beautiful. One might fancy it the notes of an organ," murmured Pascalon, who, with moist eyes, was in ecstasy like a saint in a stained-glass window. Excourbaniès shouted without any fear, and the echo repeated itself in his Tarascon dialect until it finally died away: "Ha! ha! ha! *fen dé brut!*"

But they got tired of this in about two hours, proceeding through the same scenery— was it all arranged? — green on blue; glaciers at the bottom; and as sonorous as a musical clock. The roar of the torrents, the three-voice choruses, the sellers of wood-carvings, the little flower-girls, became insupportable to our friends: the dampness, too, the steam at the bottom of this gorge, the humid ground, full of water-plants, into which the sun never penetrates.

"It is enough to give one pleurisy," remarked Bravida, pulling up his coat-collar. Then fatigue, hunger, and ill-humour all attacked him at once. They could find no inn, and, being stuffed with raspberries, Excourbaniès and Bravida began to suffer cruelly. Even Pascalon himself—that angel—laden not only with the flag, but with the ice-axe, the sac, and the alpenstock, of which the others had by turns disembarrassed themselves, had lost his sprightliness and activity.

At a turn of the road, as they were about to cross the Lutschine on one of the covered bridges which are found in very snowy districts, a very formidable blowing of a horn reached their ears.

"Ah! *vé!* enough! enough!" screamed the exasperated delegation.

The blower—a giant ambushed by the side of the road—put down an enormous pine-trumpet, which rested on the ground and was terminated by a sounding-box which gave to this prehistoric instrument the loudness of a piece of artillery.

"Ask him whether he knows where there is an inn?" said the President to Excourbaniès, who with great dignity, and with a very small pocket-dictionary, pretended to act as interpreter to the delegation since they were in German Switzerland. But before he could produce his dictionary, the horn-blower replied in very good French:

"An inn, gentlemen? why, certainly: the *Chamois fidèle* is quite close by: allow me to show you the way?"

And while he accompanied them thither he informed them that he had lived in Paris many years as commissionaire at the corner of the Rue Vivienne.

"Another of the Company's people, *parbleu!*" thought Tartarin, leaving his friends to be amazed. The *confrère* of Bompard also made himself very useful, for although the sign of the house was in French, the people of the *Chamois fidèle* only spoke a horrible German *patois*.

The delegates, seated before an enormous potato omelette, soon recovered their health and good humour, which are essential to the Southerner as the sun is to his country. They drank deeply, and ate well. After toasts drunk to the President and to his ascent, Tartarin, who had been much exercised in his mind concerning the sign, turned to the horn-player, who was breaking a crust in the same room with them, and said:

"So you have some chamois hereabouts? I thought none were left in Switzerland."

The man winked his eyes:

"There are not many of them, but we could manage to let you see one all the same!"

"He wants to shoot at one, *vé!*" said Pascalon enthusiastically, "and the President never misses his aim."

Tartarin was sorry he had not brought his gun.

"Wait a minute; I will speak to the 'patron.'"

He ascertained that the innkeeper was an old chamois-hunter; he offered his gun, powder, his buckshot, and even his services as guide to the gentlemen, towards a lair which he knew.

"*En avant: zou!*" cried Tartarin, yielding to his Alpinists, who were delighted to witness their chief's skill. It was only a trifling delay after all; and the Jungfrau would lose nothing by waiting.

Leaving the inn by the back door, they had only to push through a path in an orchard scarcely larger than the little garden of a station-master on a railway, to find themselves on the mountain side, cut up by great crevasses between the pines and the bushes.

The innkeeper had gone on ahead, and the delegates could perceive him gesticulating and throwing stones, no doubt with a view to startling the animal. They had considerable trouble to rejoin him on the rocky and difficult slopes, particularly for people who have just got up from table, and who are no more accustomed to climbing than the worthy Tarasconnais were. There was, besides, a heavy air, a pressage of storm, which rolled the clouds slowly across the peaks overhead.

"*Boufre!*" whined Bravida.

Excourbaniès groaned:

"*Outre!*"

"Let me tell you—" added the tame and bleating Pascalon.

But as the guide motioned them to be silent and to stay where they were, they obeyed. "One should never speak when carrying arms," said Tartarin of Tarascon with a severity of which each took his share, although the President was the only one armed. They remained standing and holding their breath; suddenly Pascalon exclaimed: "*Vé!* the chamois*!* *Vé!*"

At a hundred yards above them there stood the pretty animal, his horns upright, his coat a pretty fawn colour, the four feet planted together upon a rock. It was plainly visible against the sky, looking around without any appearance of fear. Tartarin methodically shouldered his gun as usual: he was going to fire, when the chamois disappeared!

"It is your fault," said the Commandant to Pascalon. "You whistled—that frightened it."

"I whistled! I!"

"Then it was Spiridion."

"Ah! *vaï;* I never whistled in my life."

There had nevertheless been a whistle, shrill and long. The President put them all at their ease by informing them that the chamois at the approach of an enemy utters a whistling noise through his nostrils. What a devil of a fellow Tartarin was! he knew all the details of chamois-hunting as well as of all the other sports. At the guide's suggestion they continued their way; but the slope became more and more steep, the rocks more uneven, with sloughs and gullies to right and left. Tartarin kept his presence of mind, turning round every moment to assist the delegates, to hold out his hand or his gun to them.

"The hand, the hand! if it's all the same to you," exclaimed the brave Bravida, who had a mortal horror of loaded firearms.

Another sign from the guide—another halt.

"I think I felt a drop of rain," muttered the Commandant, who was very anxious. At the same time it thundered, and louder than the thunder rose the voice of Excourbaniès: "Look out, Tartarin!" The chamois came on, bounding between them like a flash—too quick for even Tartarin to shoulder his gun, not quick enough though to prevent them from hearing the loud whistling of his nostrils.

"I will give an account of him, *coquin de*

"Tartarin shouldered his gun methodically as usual."

sort!" said the President; but the delegates protested. Excourbaniès suddenly very sharply asked him if he had sworn to exterminate them.

"Dear ma-as-ter," bleated Pascalon, timidly, "I have heard it said that the chamois when driven to bay turns against the hunter, and becomes very dangerous."

"Don't let us bring him to bay, then," said Bravida the terrible.

Tartarin called them chicken-hearted milksops. Then suddenly, while they were disputing, they lost sight of each other in a thick, warm cloud which smelt of sulphur, and through which they kept searching for each other, calling out :

"*Hé!* Tartarin!"

"Are you there, Placide!"

"Ma-as-ter!"

"Keep cool! keep cool!"

There was a regular panic. Then a gust of wind dispersed the cloud, carried it away like a veil torn off the bushes, and from it came a forked flash of lightning, followed by an awful crash of thunder under their very feet as it seemed.

"My cap!" exclaimed Spiridion, whose hair was standing up quite electrified, his head-gear having been carried off by the tempest. They were in the heart of the storm—in Vulcan's forge itself. Bravida first fled at full speed; the remainder of the delegation followed him; but one cry from the P. C. A., who thought for them all, restrained them:

"*Malheureux!* beware of the lightning!"

Besides, outside of the real dangers which threatened them, they could scarcely run upon the steep slopes, across ravines now transformed into torrents and cascades by the rain. Their return was disastrous, at a slow pace, amid the lightning, the thunder, their tumbles, *glissades*, and forced halts. Pascalon crossed himself, and appealed aloud as at Tarascon to Saint Martha, Saint Helena, and Saint Mary Magdalen, while Excourbaniès swore "*Coquin de sort!*" and Bravida, who brought up the rear, turning round in a nervous state, said:

"What is that I hear coming behind us? that sniffling, that gallop,—there—it has stopped!" The idea of the maddened chamois throwing itself upon the hunters could not be banished from the mind of the old warrior. In a low tone, so as not to alarm the others, he imparted his fears to Tartarin, who bravely changed places with him, and marched last with head held high, wet to the skin, yet with the inward determination which imminent danger bestows! But when they had regained the inn, and when he saw his dear Alpinists in shelter, in a fair way to dry themselves around an enormous faïence stove, in a room on the first floor, whence was ascending the odour of hot grog and wine, then the President felt himself shiver, and he declared with a very pale face: "I really believe I am taken ill."

Taken ill! an expression of sinister meaning in its vagueness and brevity, which hinted at all kinds of maladies—plague, cholera, yellow fever, "blue devils," jaundice, and lightning-strokes, the thought of which always occurred to the Tarasconnais at the least indisposition.

Tartarin was taken ill! There could, therefore, be no question of continuing the journey, and the delegates only cared for rest. Quickly they warmed his bed, plied him with wine,

and at the second glass the President felt a grateful warmth permeate his body: a good omen! Two pillows at his back, an eider-down on his feet, his comforter tied over his head, he experienced a delicious satisfaction in listening to the roarings of the storm; in the pleasant smell of the pines; in the little rustic, wooden inn, with latticed windows; in regarding his friends, the dear Alpinists, who pressed around his bed, glasses in hand, looking such queer figures in their odd costumes of curtains and such materials, with their Gallic, Saracen, or Roman types of features, while their clothes were drying before the stove. Forgetting himself, he questioned them in a doleful voice:

"Are you quite well, Placide? Spiridion, you seemed to be unwell just now."

No, Spiridion suffered no longer, it had all passed away when the President was taken so ill. Bravida, who suited the moral to the proverbs of his country, added cynically: "The sickness of a neighbour comforts and even cures us." Then they spoke of their hunting, warming at the recollection of certain dangerous incidents, such as when the animal had turned upon them furiously; and without any complicity of lying, they very ingeniously fabricated a fable which they would relate on their return.

Suddenly, Pascalon, who had gone down stairs for another modicum of grog, reappeared in the greatest alarm—a naked arm outside his blue-flowered curtain, which he gathered around him with modest gesture *à la Polyeucte*. He was more than a second in the room before he could utter in a low voice and with quick breathing:

"The chamois!"

"Well, what about it?"

"It is down stairs, in the kitchen!"

"Ah, go along!"

"You are joking!"

"Will you go and see, Placide?"

Bravida hesitated; so Excourbaniès descended on tip-toe; and then returned almost immediately, with a scared face. More extraordinary news still—

The chamois was drinking warm wine!

They owed him as much, poor beast, after the pretended hunt he had afforded them on the mountain, all the time started off or recalled by his master, who usually contented himself with putting it through its paces in the *salle* to show tourists how easily it had been tamed.

"This is crushing," said Bravida, not caring to understand any more about it, while Tartarin pulled the comforter over his face to hide from the delegates the gentle mirth which overspread his features, when at any stage of his journey he encountered the all-satisfying Switzerland of Bompard, with its mechanism and its supernumeraries!

X

The ascent of the Jungfrau.—Vé! the oxen!—The Kennedy "crampons" do not answer; neither does the lamp.—Appearance of masked men at the chalet - The President in the crevasse.—He leaves his spectacles behind him.—On the peaks.—Tartarin a deity.

THERE was a tremendous crowd that morning at the Belle Vue Hotel on the Little Scheideck. Notwithstanding the rain and the squalls, the tables had been laid out of doors, under the shelter of the veranda, amongst an assemblage of alpenstocks, flasks, telescopes, cuckoo-clocks, &c.; and the tourists could, while breakfasting, gaze to the left upon the valley of Grindelwald, some 6,000 feet below; on the right the Lauterbrunnen valley, and in front of them, at what seemed within gun-shot distance, the pure and stupendous slopes of the Jungfrau, with its *névé*, its glaciers, the whiteness of it all illuminating the air around, making the glasses still more transparent and the table-linen still more snowy.

But for the moment the attention of the company was directed to a noisy bearded party of tourists, who were coming up on mule-back, on donkey-back, one man even in a *chaise à porteurs*, who prepared themselves for the ascent by a copious breakfast; they were in high spirits, and the noise they made contrasted greatly with the worn-out and solemn airs of the Rice and Prune factions, some illustrious members of which had assembled at the Scheideck: Lord Chippendale, the Belgian Senator and his family, the Austro-Hungarian diplomatist and his family. It seemed as if all these bearded people were about to attempt the ascent, for they occupied themselves in turn with the preparations for departure, rose, hurried off to give instructions to the guides; to inspect the provisions, and from one end of the terrace to the other they shouted to each other in discordant accents:

"*Hé!* Placide, see if the frying-pan is in the bag, and don't forget the spirit-lamp, mind!"

When the starting time arrived, however, it was perceived that all this was on account of one, and that of all the party one individual alone was going to undertake the ascent! But what an individual!

"Children, are we ready?" said the good Tartarin, in a triumphant and joyful tone, which did not tremble with the shadow of a fear for the possible perils of the journey, his last doubt concerning the "machinery" of the Swiss having been dissipated that morning before the two Grindelwald glaciers, each provided with a turn-stile and a *guichet* with an inscription, "Entrance to the glacier, one franc and a half."

He could then enjoy this departure without regret: the delight of feeling himself the observed of all observers; envied, admired, by those cheeky little girls with the close-cropped hair, who had laughed at him so

quietly on the Rigi-Kulm ; and who were at that very moment in raptures, comparing that little man with that enormous mountain which he was going to ascend. One was sketching him in her album, another was requesting the honour of holding his alpenstock. "Tchimppegne — Tchimppegne," suddenly cried a lanky, melancholy Englishman, of brick-tint, who was approaching with a bottle and a

glass in his hands. Then, after having compelled the hero to drink, he said:

"Lord Chippendale, sir; *et tô!*"

"Tartarin de Tarascon."

"Oh, yes,—Tarterine. It's a capital name for a horse," said his lordship, who must have been a great sportsman on the other side of the Channel!

The Austro-Hungarian diplomatist also came forward to shake the mountaineer by the hand between his mittens having a vague recollection of having met him somewhere. "Delighted, delighted," he repeated many times, and, not knowing how to get out of it, he added : " My compliments to Madame," —his society formula, by which he concluded all introductions.

But the guides were becoming impatient. The cabin of the Alpine Club must be reached before dark ; there they would sleep, and there was not a moment to lose. Tartarin quite understood this, and saluted the company with a wave of his hand, smiled paternally at the malicious "misses," and then, in a voice of thunder, cried:

" Pascalon, the banner ! "

It was displayed, the Southerners had unfolded it, for they like theatrical display ; and at the thirtieth repetition of " *Vive le Président!*" " *Vive Tartarin!*" " Ha ! ha ! *feu dé brut*," the party started—the two guides in front carrying the *sac*, the provisions, and some wood ; then Pascalon, holding the "oriflamme;" and the P. C. A. with the delegates, who were to escort him to the Guggi glacier, brought up the rear. So the procession deployed, the folds of the flag flapping upon the swampy ground, or on the naked or snowy crests, the *cortège* in a vague way recalling *le jour des morts* in country places.

Suddenly, the Commandant cried out in great alarm:

"*Vé!* oxen!"

They perceived some cattle grazing amid the undulations of the ground. The old warrior had a nervous terror of cows—an insurmountable fear; and as his friends could not leave him alone, the delegation was obliged to halt. Pascalon handed the banner to one of the guides; then a last embrace, a few hurried words of warning, with their eyes on the cows:

"Adieu, *qué!*"

"No imprudence, mind!"

And they parted.

As for any one proposing to ascend with the President, it was not to be thought of. The ascent was too high, *boufre!* As one got nearer to it, it seemed more difficult, the ravines increased, the peaks bristled up in a white chaos which seemed impossible to traverse. It was much better worth while to watch the ascent from the Sheideck.

Naturally, Tartarin in all his life had never set foot on a glacier. There were no such things upon the hillocks of Tarascon, which were as perfumed and dry as a bundle of bent-grass. Yet the surroundings of the Guggi gave him a sensation of familiarity, as if he had seen them before— arousing the memory of the chase in Provence, all around the Camargue, towards the sea. It was the same grass, but shorter and burnt up as if scorched by fire. Here and there were pools of water, infiltrations, indicated by slim reeds; then the moraine, like a mobile hill of sand, broken shells, and cinders; then the glacier, with its blue-green waves, tipped with white, undulating as a silent and frozen sea. The wind also had all the coolness and freshness of the sea-breeze.

"No, thanks; I have my *crampons*," said Tartarin, as the guide offered him woollen foot-protectors to wear over his boots: "Kennedy's pattern *crampons*—first-rate—very convenient." He shouted all this at the top of his voice as if the guide were deaf, so as to make him understand better, for Christian Inebnit knew no more French than his comrade Kaufmann. Then Tartarin

seated himself upon the moraine and fixed upon his boots with irons the species of large pointed iron socks called *crampons*.

He had experimented a hundred times with these "Kennedy *crampons*," and had tried them in the garden where the baobab grew; nevertheless the result was unexpected. Beneath the hero's weight the spikes buried themselves in the ice to such a depth that all attempts to extricate them were vain ! Behold Tartarin nailed to the ice, springing, swearing, making semaphores of his arms and alpenstock; and finally reduced to recall his guides, who had gone on ahead in the full belief that they had to do with an experienced climber !

Finding it impossible to pull him up, they unfastened the *crampons* from him, and left them in the ice, replacing them by a pair of worsted boot-coverings. The President then continued his way, not without toil and fatigue. Unaccustomed to use his *bâton*, he knocked it against his legs; the iron slid away from him, dragging him with it, when he leaned on it too heavily; then he tried the ice-axe, which proved even more difficult to manage; the swellings of the glacier increased, casting up its motionless waves into the appearance of a furious ocean suddenly petrified.

Apparently motionless only—for the loud crackings, the interior rumblings, the enormous blocks of ice slowly displaced like the revolving scenes at a theatre, displayed the action, the treacherousness, of this immense glacial mass; and before the climber's eyes, within reach of his axe, crevasses opened—bottomless pits into which the pieces of ice rolled to infinity. The hero fell into many of these traps—once up to his waist into one of the green gulfs, wherein his broad shoulders alone prevented him from being buried.

Seeing him so unskilful, and at the same time so calm and collected—laughing, singing, gesticulating, just as he had been doing at breakfast—the guides began to think that the Swiss champagne had got into his head. Could they think anything else of a President of an Alpine Club, of a mountaineer so renowned, of whom his companions never spoke without "Ah!" and expressive gestures? Having, therefore, seized him under his arms after the respectful fashion of policemen putting a well-born but elevated young gentleman into a cab, the guides, by the aid of monosyllables and gestures, endeavoured to arouse his reason to the dangers of the route: the threatening appearance of the crevasses, the cold, and the avalanches. With the points of their ice-axes they indicated the enormous accumulations of ice, the sloping wall of *névé* in front, rising to the zenith in a blinding glare.

But the worthy Tartarin laughed at all this. "*Ah! vaï, les crevasses!* Ah! get out with your avalanches!" and he choked with laughter, winked at the guides, and nudged them playfully in the ribs, to make them understand that he was in the secret as well as they!

The men ended by joining in the fun, carried away by Tarascon melody; and when they rested a moment upon a block of ice to permit "*monsieur*" to take breath, they "jodelled" in Swiss fashion, but not loudly, for fear of avalanches, nor for long, because time was passing apace. Evening was evidently coming on, the cold was becoming more intense, and the singular discoloration of the snows and the ice, heaped up and overhanging in masses, which, even under a cloudy sky, glitter and sparkle, but when daylight is dying out, gone up towards the tapering peaks, take the livid, spectral tints of the lunar world. Pallor, congelation, silence — all is dead. And the good Tartarin, so warm, so lively, began at length to lose his *verve*, when at the distant cry of a bird, the call of the "snow partridge" (ptarmigan) resounding

amid the desolation, before his eyes there passed a vision of a burnt-up country, browned under a setting sun, sportsmen of Tarascon, wiping their foreheads, seated upon their empty game-bags, beneath the shade of an olive-tree ! This reminiscence comforted him.

At the same time Kaufmann was pointing out to him something above them which looked like a faggot on the snow. This was the hut. It seemed as if a few paces would suffice to reach it, but it was a good half-hour ere they got there. One of the guides went on in front to light the fire. It was dark by this time; the east wind came piercingly off the death-like ground, and Tartarin, no longer troubling himself about anything, firmly sustained by the arm of the guide, jumped and bounded about until there was not a dry thread on him, notwithstanding the lowness of the temperature. Suddenly, a savoury odour of onion-soup assailed their nostrils.

They had reached the hut.

Nothing can be more simple than these stopping-places established on the mountains by the forethought of the Swiss Alpine Club : a single room, in which a sloping plank, serving as bed-place, occupies nearly all the space, leaving very little for the stove and the long table, which is nailed to the floor, as well as the benches which surround it. The supper was already laid when the men arrived ; three bowls, tin spoons, the " Etna" for the coffee, two tins of Chicago preserved meats opened. Tartarin found the dinner excellent, although the onion-soup was rather smoked, and the famous patent lamp, which ought to have produced a quart of coffee in three minutes, failed to work.

For dessert they sang : it was the only way to converse with the guides. He sang his country's songs : *la Tarasque, les Filles d'Avignon*. The guides responded with local songs in their German *patois :* " *Mi Vater isch en Appenzeller ; aou, aou !* " Fine fellows these— hard as rock, with soft flowing beards like moss, clear eyes, accustomed to move in space, as sailors' are ; and this sensation of the sea and space, which he had lately experienced while ascending the Guggi, Tartarin again experienced here in the company of these glacier-pilots in that narrow cabin, low and smoky, a veritable "'tween-decks," in the dripping of the snow which the heat had melted on the roof, and the wild gusts of wind, like masses of falling water, shaking everything, making the planks creak and the lamp flicker: then suddenly stopping in a silence as if all the world were dead.

Dinner was finished, when heavy steps were heard approaching, and voices were distinguished. A violent knocking at the door! Tartarin, somewhat alarmed, gazed at the guides. A nocturnal attack at such an elevation as this? The blows redoubled in intensity. "Who is there?" cried the hero, seizing his ice-axe: but the cabin was already invaded by two tall Americans masked in white linen, their clothing saturated with perspiration and snow-water, and behind them guides and porters—quite a caravan coming down from the summit of the Jungfrau.

"Welcome, my lords," cried Tartarin, with a hospitable and patronising wave of his hand, but "milords" had no compunction as to making themselves quite at home. In a few seconds the table was relaid, the bowls and spoons passed through some hot water to serve for the new-comers, according to the rules existing in all Alpine huts, the boots of "milords" were drying at the stove, while they, with their feet wrapped in straw, were disposing of a new supply of onion-soup.

These Americans were father and son — two ruddy giants, with the heads of pioneers, hard and practical. The older of the two seemed to have white eyes; and after awhile the manner in which he tapped and felt around him, and the care which his son took of him, assured Tartarin that he was the famous blind mountaineer of whom he had heard at the Belle Vue Hotel, a fact he could scarcely credit, a famous climber in his youth, and who, notwithstanding his sixty years, had recommenced his ascents again with his son. He had in this manner already made the ascent of the Wetterhorn and the Jungfrau, and reckoned upon attacking the Cervin and Mont Blanc, declaring that the mountain air gave him intense enjoyment, and recalled all his former vigour.

"But," said Tartarin to one of the porters —for the Yankees were not communicative, and only replied "Yes" or "No" to all advances—"but, if he cannot see, how can he manage to cross dangerous places?"

"Oh, he has the foot of a true mountaineer, and his son looks after him, places his feet in the proper positions, &c. The fact is, he never has an accident."

"More especially as accidents are never very deplorable, *qué?*" After a knowing smile to the astonished porter, the Tarasconnais, more and more persuaded that all this was *blague*, stretched himself on the plank, rolled himself in his rug, his comforter up to his eyes, and fell asleep, notwithstanding the light, the chatter, the smoke of pipes, and the smell of the onion-soup.

"*Mossié! Mossié!*" (Monseiur).

One of the guides was shaking him by the shoulder, while the other was pouring out some boiling coffee into the bowls. There were a few oaths and some grumbling from the sleepers, as Tartarin pushed past them in his way to the table and to the door. All of a sudden, he found himself in the open air, shivering with cold, and puzzled by the moonlight upon the white plains, the frozen cascades, which the shadows of the peaks, *aiguilles*, and *séracs*, cut with intense blackness. There was not the bewildering scintillation of the afternoon, nor the livid grey tinge of the evening, but a town cut by dark alleys, mysterious passages, dubious angles between the marble monuments and crumbled ruins—a dead town with its wide deserted squares.

Two o'clock! With good walking they ought to reach the summit by mid-day. "*Zou*," said the P. C. A. quite gaily, and pressed forward to the assault. But the guides stopped him: it was necessary to rope themselves.

"Ah! go along with your tying up! Very well, then; if it amuses you, be it so!"

Christian Inebnit took the lead, leaving six feet of rope between him and Tartarin, and the same length between Tartarin and the other guide, who was carrying the provisions and the banner. The Tarasconnais got on better than the day before, and really he did not seem to appreciate the difficulties of the path—if the way along that terrible *arête* of ice can be called a path—over which they were advancing with the greatest caution. It was a few inches wide, and so slippery that Christian had to cut steps in it.

The *arête* glittered between profound abysses. But do you think Tartarin was afraid? Not a bit of it! Scarcely did he experience the little tremor of the newly-made Freemason who has to submit to the ordeal! He placed his feet exactly in the holes cut by the guide, doing everything as he saw him do it, as coolly as if he were in the baobab garden, walking on the edge of the fountain, to the great terror of the gold-fish. At one time, the crest became so narrow that they were compelled to proceed on all-fours, and while they were advancing slowly a tremendous detonation was heard on the right beneath them. "An avalanche!" said Inebnit, stopping quite still so long as the uproar lasted, while the reverberations, grandly repeated, terminated by a lengthened thunder-roll, which slowly died away in echoes. After that the former terrible silence succeeded, covering all things like a winding-sheet.

The *arête* passed, they reached the *névé*, which sloped easily, but was terribly long. They had climbed for more than an hour, when a thin streak of rosy hue began to touch the peaks high—very high—over their heads. Day was announcing its arrival. As a good Southerner, cherishing an enmity to darkness, Tartarin trolled out his cheerful song:

> *Grand souleù de la Prouvenço
> Gai compaire dou mistrau.*[1]

A tug at the cord both before and behind stopped him short in the middle of his verse:

---

[1] Grand soleil de la Provence,—Gai compère du mistral.

"Hush! hush!" cried Inebnit, indicating with the handle of his ice-axe the menacing line of immense and clustered *séracs* which the least shock would send down upon the travellers. But the Tarasconnais knew what he was about—they were not going to humbug him; so he recommenced in a resonant voice:

> *Tu qu'escoulès la Duranço*
> *Commo un flot dé vin de Crau.*[1]

The guides, perceiving that they could not keep the headstrong singer within due bounds, made a wide *détour* to avoid the *séracs*, and soon were brought to a standstill by an enormous *crevasse*, which was lighted in its green depths by the first rays of daylight. A snow bridge crossed it, but so thin and fragile, that at the very first step it disappeared in a whirlwind of fine snow, dragging with it the head guide and Tartarin, who hung by the cord, which Rudolf Kaufmann, the rear guide, gripped with all his force, his axe firmly fixed in the snow to sustain the tension. But

---

[1] Toi qui siffles la Durance—Comme un coup de vin de Crau.

though he could hold up the men, he could not haul them out, and he stood crouching down, with clenched teeth and straining muscles, too far from the *crevasse* to perceive what was passing within it.

Astounded by the fall, and half blinded by the snow, Tartarin for a minute threw his legs and arms about like a puppet: but then, righting himself by means of the rope, he hung over the chasm, his nose touching the icy wall, which thawed beneath his breathing, in the posture of a plumber mending a water-pipe. He saw the sky paling above him, the last stars were disappearing; beneath him a chasm of intense darkness, whence ascended a cold air.

Nevertheless, his first astonishment over, he regained his coolness and good humour:

"Eh! up there! Father Kaufmann, don't let us get mouldy here, *què!* There is a draught, and this cursed cord is bruising our ribs."

Kaufmann was not able to reply. If he unlocked his teeth he would lose some of his strength. But Inebnit hailed from below:

"*Mossié! Mossié!* ice-axe!"—for he had lost his own in the *crevasse;* and the heavy instrument passed from Tartarin's hands into those of the guide--a difficult operation because of the length of cord which separated them. The guide wanted it to cut steps in the ice in front of him, or to cling by it foot and hand.

The strain upon the rope being thus lessened by one half, Rudolf Kaufmann, with carefully calculated force and infinite precautions, commenced to drag up the President, whose cap at length appeared over the edge of the *crevasse*. Inebnit came up in his turn, and the two mountaineers met with effusion, but with the few words which are exchanged after great dangers by people of a slow habit of speaking. They were much moved, and trembling with their exertions. Tartarin passed them his flask to restore them. He seemed quite composed and calm, and while he was beating the snow from his dress rhythmically, he kept humming a tune, under the very noses of the astonished guides.

"*Brav! brav! Franzose,*" said Kaufmann,

patting him on the shoulder, and Tartarin, with his jolly laugh, replied :

"*Farceur*, I knew quite well there was no danger!"

Within the memory of guide, never had there been such an Alpinist as this!

They continued their way, climbing a gigantic wall of ice eighteen hundred or two thousand feet high, in which they cut steps, which occupied much time.

The man of Tarascon began to feel his strength failing him under the blazing sun, which reflected all the whiteness of the landscape, all the more trying for his eyes as he had dropped his spectacles into the *crevasse*. Soon afterwards a terrible faintness seized upon him, that "*mal de montagnes*" which has the same effect as sea-sickness. Utterly done up, and light-headed, with dragging limbs, he stumbled about, so that the guides had to haul him along, one on each side, as they had done the day before, sustaining him, even drawing him up the ice-wall. Scarcely three hundred feet intervened between them and the top of the Jungfrau; but although the snow was firm and the way easy, this last stage occupied an "interminable" time, while the fatigue and the sensation of suffocation increased with Tartarin continually.

Suddenly, the guides let him go, and waving their hats began to "jodel" with delight. They had reached the summit. This point in immaculate space, this white crest somewhat rounded, was the end, and for poor Tartarin the end of the torpor in which he had been walking, as in his sleep, for the last hour.

"Scheideck! Scheideck!" exclaimed the guides, pointing out to him far below on a verdant plateau, standing out from the mists of the valley, the Hôtel Belle Vue, looking a very toy-house.

From there they had a magnificent panorama spread before them, a snow slope tinged with an orange glow by the sun, or a cold deep blue; a mass of ice fantastically sculptured into towers, steeples, needles, *arêtes;* gigantic mounds, like graves of the mastodon and the megatherium. All the colours of the rainbow played upon them, uniting again in the beds of the great glaciers, with their motionless ice-falls, crossed by tiny streams which the sun was warming into life again. But at that great elevation the reflections were toned down, a light was floating in the air, a cold ecliptic light, which made Tartarin shiver as much as the sensation of the silence and solitude of the white desert and its mysterious recesses.

A little smoke was perceived, and some detonations were heard from the hotel. They had seen the tourists, and were firing cannon in their honour, and the conviction that they saw him, that his Alpinists were there, the young ladies, the illustrious Rices and Prunes, with their opera-glasses, recalled Tartarin to the importance of his mission. He snatched the Tarascon banner from the hands of the guide, and waved it two or three times; then, fixing his ice-axe in the snow, he seated himself upon the iron of the pick, flag in hand, superb, facing the public. And without his perceiving it—by one of those spectral images frequent at the tops of mountains, the result of sun, and of mist which was rising behind him—a gigantic Tartarin was outlined on the sky, enlarged and shortened, the beard bristling out of the comforter, like one of the Scandinavian deities, which tradition presents to us as enthroned in the midst of the clouds.

XI

*En route for Tarascon!—The Lake of Geneva.
—Tartarin suggests a visit to Bonnivard's
cell.—A short dialogue amid the roses.—All
the band under lock and key.—The unfortunate Bonnivard.—A certain rope made in
Avignon comes to light.*

AFTER the ascent, Tartarin's nose peeled
and became pimpled, his cheeks cracked.
He was obliged to remain in his room for
five days at the Belle Vue. Five days of compresses, pomades of which he whiled away
the cloying mawkishness and boredom by
making little whist parties with the delegates,

or dictating to them a long detailed account, most circumstantial in incidents, of his expedition, to be read in full meeting at the club, and published in the *Forum*. Then, when his general fatigue had abated, and there remained upon the noble features of the P. C. A. a few blisters, scars, and cracks, with a beautiful Etruscan vase tint, the delegation and its President took the route for Tarascon *via* Geneva.

Let us pass over the incidents of the journey: the terror which the Southern party aroused in the narrow railway-carriages, the steamers, the *tables d'hôte*, by their songs, cries, and their exuberant affection for each other; their banner, and their alpenstocks, for since the ascent of the P. C. A. they had all furnished themselves with stocks, on which the records of celebrated ascents were burnt in black letters.

Montreux!

Here the delegates, at the suggestion of their leader, decided to halt for two or three days, to see the celebrated shores of the Lake Leman particularly Chillon, and the legendary prison in which languished the great patriot Bonnivard, as related by Byron and Delacroix.

As for Tartarin, he cared very little for Bonnivard; his adventure with William Tell had enlightened him concerning Swiss legends; but while passing through Interlachen he had learnt that Sonia was about to leave for Montreux with her brother, whose condition had become more serious, and this invention of a pilgrimage served him as a pretext to see the young lady once more, and—who knows?—to persuade her to follow him to Tarascon.

It must be understood that his followers all believed in the good faith of their leader when he said he came to render homage to the celebrated citizen of Geneva, whose story the P. C. A. had related; even now, with their taste for theatrical display, they would have marched in line to Chillon, with the banner displayed, crying " *Vive Bonnivard!* " But the President was obliged to restrain them. " Let us first breakfast," he said, " and then we shall see."

They filled the omnibus of a *pension* Müller, situated, like many others, near the landing stage by the lake.

"*Vé! le gendarme!* How he stares at us," said Pascalon, as last of all he got into the

omnibus with the banner, which was very much in the way; and Bravida, who was nervous, said: "That's true; what can that *gendarme* want with us that he examines us so closely?"

"Perhaps he recognises me, *pardi!*" said the good Tartarin, and he smiled a far off smile at the Vaudois policeman, whose long blue *capote* was persistently turned towards the omnibus, which was proceeding along the poplar-lined road by the lake side.

That was market-day in Montreux. Rows

of little shops in the open air were ranged along the lake, filled with fruit, vegetables, cheap lace, and with the silver jewellery, chains, *plaques*, brooches, &c., which embellish the Swiss female costumes like "worked" snow or ice-pearls. Amid these shops flowed the stream of people from the little harbour, which sheltered a flotilla of boats of brilliant colours, and where the disembarkation of bags and barrels from the vessels with antennæ-like sails, the shrill whistling, the bells of the steamers, the bustle of the *cafés*, the beer-shops, the florists, and the second-hand dealers which line the quay, were continually mingling. With a little sun, one might have fancied one's self in some Mediterranean port, between Mentone and Bordighera. But the sun was wanting, and the natives of Tarascon looked at this pretty country through a veil of water which rose from the blue lake, climbed up the stony streets, united above the houses with other clouds, massed amid the dark verdure of the mountains, charged with rain, and ready to burst.

"*Coquin de sort!* I am not a lake-man," said Spiridion Excourbaniès, rubbing the glass of the omnibus window to see the views of the glaciers.

"No more am I," sighed Pascalon; "this fog, this dead water, makes one inclined to weep."

Bravida complained also: he was afraid of his sciatica.

Tartarin reprimanded them severely. Was

it, then, nothing that they would be able to say, when they returned, that they had seen the prison of Bonnivard, written their names on the historic walls beside the signatures of Rousseau, Byron, Victor Hugo, George Sand, Eugène Sue? Suddenly, in the middle of this tirade, the President interrupted himself—changed colour. He had seen a little *toque*, resting on blonde hair, passing by. Without even stopping the omnibus, just then slackening for the ascent, he leaped out, saying, "Go on to the hotel," to the stupefied Alpinists.

"Sonia! Sonia!"

He was afraid he would not be able to overtake her, so hurried was she, her slim shadow flitting along the wall of the road. She turned and waited for him: "Ah! 'tis you!" Immediately their hands clasped she resumed her walk. He placed himself beside her, out of breath, excusing himself for having quitted her in such sudden fashion —the arrival of his friends—the necessity for the ascent, of which his face still bore the traces. She listened without saying a word, hurrying on, her eyes fixed and wide open. Judging by her profile, she seemed to him pale, her features deprived of their infantine candour, with something hard, resolute, which until then had not existed, but in her voice - her imperious will; but still her juvenile gracefulness, her waving, golden hair!

"And Boris—how is he?" asked Tartarin, a little put out by her silence, by the coldness which was creeping over him.

"Boris?" She trembled. "Ah! yes, it is true; you didn't know. Well, then, come with me; come."

They proceeded along a little path, bordered with vines hanging almost over the lake, and

"The little cemetery amidst the roses, on the border of the lake."

villas, gardens—sanded, elegant, the terraces planted with the virgin vine, roses, petunias, and myrtle. From time to time they passed some strange face, with troubled features and mournful looks, their steps slow and melancholy, such as one meets with at Mentone or Monaco : only there the light devours all, absorbs everything ; while beneath the cloudy sky suffering is more apparent, while the flowers appear fresher.

"Come in," said Sonia, pushing open a gate beneath a pediment of white masonry, inscribed with Russian characters in golden letters.

Tartarin did not at first understand where he was. A little garden with carefully tended walks, pebbly, full of climbing roses amid the green bushes, great clusters of yellow and white blossoms filled the place with their aroma and bloom. Amongst these garlands, this marvellous display of blossom, were some stones standing up or lying down, with dates and names upon them, this one, quite new :

"*Boris de Wassilief, aged 22 years.*"

He had been laid there for some days, having

died almost immediately after he had reached Montreux; and, in this cemetery of strangers, he found a trace of his native land amongst the Russians, Poles, Swedes, buried beneath the flowers - consumptive patients who are sent to this northern Nice, because the sunny South is too hot, and the transition too sudden for them.

The pair remained motionless and silent for a moment before the new white headstone on the dark ground of the freshly-turned earth: the young girl, with bowed head, breathing the odour of the abundant roses, and thus resting her swollen eyes.

"Poor little thing!" said Tartarin, much affected; and, taking in his strong rough hands the tips of Sonia's fingers, he continued: "And you? What will become of you, now?"

She looked him full in the face with dry and brilliant eyes, in which no tear trembled:

"I? I leave here in an hour!"

"You are going away?"

"Bolibine is already in St. Petersburg. Maniloff is waiting for me to pass the frontier.

I am about to enter the furnace. People will hear us talked about." Then, in an undertone, she added, with a half smile, fixing her blue eyes full on the face of Tartarin, who blanched and avoided her gaze: "Who loves me will follow me!"

Ah! *vaï*, follow her! This enthusiast made him afraid; besides, this funereal scene had cooled his ardour. He struggled, nevertheless, not to run away like a contemptible wretch. So, with his hand on his heart, and a gesture worthy of Abenceragus, the hero began: "You know me, Sonia——"

She did not wish to hear any more.

"Babbler!" she replied, shrugging her shoulders. And then she left him, upright and proud, passing between the rose bushes without once turning round. "Babbler!" not another word, but the intonation was so contemptuous that the good Tartarin blushed under his beard, and convinced himself that they were alone in the garden, and that no one had heard them.

Fortunately, impressions did not survive long with our Tarasconnais. Five minutes

"'Babbler!' she said, with a shrug of the shoulders."

later, he ascended the terraces of Montreux with a light step, in quest of the *pension* Müller, where the Alpinists were waiting *déjeuner* for him, and he felt a great relief at the termination of this dangerous *liaison*. As he proceeded, he nodded vigorously, and explained eloquently to himself the reason which Sonia would not listen to. *Bé!* yes, it was certainly a despotism—he would not deny that; but to pass from the idea to action! *Boufre!* And then, what an employment for him, to fire upon despots! Suppose every oppressed nation came to him, as the Arabs did to Bombonnel when the panther prowled around the *douar*, all his efforts would not suffice. *Allons!*

A passing carriage quickly cut short his monologue. He had only just time to leap aside: "Look out, you animal!" But his angry exclamation was at once changed into an exclamation of surprise: "*Qués aco! Boudiou!* Impossible!" I give you a thousand guesses to divine what he saw in the landau. The delegation! The delegation in full—Bravida, Pascalon, Excourbaniès—

crowded in at one side, pale, exhausted, dishevelled, after a struggle with two *gendarmes*, muskets in hand, seated opposite to them. All their profiles, motionless, mute, in the narrow frame of the doorway, seemed like a bad dream; and Tartarin stood rooted to the spot as firmly as he ever was by the "Kennedy" *crampons*. He saw the carriage gallop off, behind it a crowd of school-boys, satchels on back, just released from school, when a voice sounded in his ear: "Here is the fourth man!' In a moment he was seized, handcuffed, bound: he was hustled into a hackney carriage with the *gendarmes* and an officer armed with his gigantic *latte*, which he held between his knees, the handle touching the top of the cab.

Tartarin wanted to speak, to explain himself. There was evidently some mistake.

He told them his name. He appealed to his Consul, to a dealer in Swiss honey who had known him at Beaucaire. Then, in face of the persistent silence of his attendants, he began to look upon this arrest as a new move of Bompard's, and, addressing himself to the officer, he said, with a waggish air: "This is all a joke, *qué!* *Ah! vaï, farceur!* I know very well it is all for fun!"

"If you speak any more I will gag you. Not a word!" said the officer, rolling his

terrible eyes, so that it seemed as if he was going to impale the prisoner on his staff.

The other kept quiet, and did not stir any more; he kept looking out of window at the borders of the lake, the high mountains—of a damp green hue—the hotels, with their varied roofs, with gilded signs visible a league away; and on the slopes, as on the Rigi, was a coming and going of men carrying up and down baskets and hods of provisions, &c.; as at the Rigi, also, a toy railway, squeaking along, and climbing up as far as Glion; and, to complete the resemblance to the *Regina montium*, a heavy beating rain was falling — an exchange of water and fog between the lake and the sky, the sky and the lake, the clouds touching the waves.

The carriage rolled over a drawbridge between some little shops where knick-knacks were sold— penknives, button-hooks, and such things; passed through a low postern, and stopped in the courtyard of an old castle, grass-grown, and flanked by round "pepper-box" towers, with black *moucharabis* supported by beams. Where was he? Tartarin understood it when he heard the officer of *gendarmes* conversing with the *concierge* of the castle, a fat man in a Grecian cap, shaking a huge bunch of rusty keys.

"In solitary confinement? But I have no room! The others occupy all — unless we put him in the Bonnivard prison."

"Put him in Bonnivard's chamber, then— it is quite good enough for him," said the captain, authoritatively. And his orders were carried out.

The Castle of Chillon, about which the President had continually been speaking to his friends the Alpinists, and in which, by the irony of fate, he found himself suddenly imprisoned without knowing why, is one of the historical monuments of Switzerland. After having served as a summer residence of the Counts of Savoy, then as a State prison, a depot of arms and stores, it is now only an excuse for an excursion, like the Rigi-Kulm or Tellsplatte. There is, however, a guard there, and a lock-up for drunkards and the wilder lads of the district; but such inmates are rare, as the Vaud is a most peaceful canton; thus the lock-up is usually untenanted, and the keeper keeps his store of fuel in it. So the arrival of all these prisoners had put him in a bad temper, particularly when he thought that people would not be able to see the celebrated dungeon, which was at that season of considerable profit.

Furious, he led the way, and Tartarin followed him, timidly, and without making any resistance. A few worn steps, a damp corridor feeling like a cave, a high door like a wall, with enormous hinges, and they found themselves in a vast subterranean vault, with deeply trodden floor, and heavy Roman pillars on which hang the rings of iron to which the State prisoners were formerly chained. A semi-daylight flickers in, and the rippling lake is reflected through the narrow apertures which permit naught but the sky to be seen.

"This is your place," said the gaoler. "Mind you don't go to the end, the *oubliettes* are there."

Tartarin recoiled in terror.

"*Les oubliettes! Boudiou!*" he exclaimed.

"What would you have, *mon garçon?* They have ordered me to put you in Bonnivard's dungeon. I have put you in Bonnivard's dungeon! Now, if you have means, I can supply you with some luxuries, such as a mattress and coverlet for the night."

"Let me have something to eat first," said Tartarin, who very fortunately had not left his purse behind him.

The *concierge* came back with some fresh bread, some beer, and a saveloy, which were all devoured eagerly by the prisoner of Chillon, who had not broken his fast since the day before, and was worn out by fatigue and emotion. While he was eating it on his stone bench in the gleam of the embrasure, the gaoler kept examining him with a good-natured air.

"*Ma foi!*" he said, "I don't know what you have done, nor why they treat you so severely."

"Eh! *coquin de sort*, no more do I! I know nothing whatever about it," replied Tartarin, with his mouth full.

"At any rate, one thing is certain— you have not the appearance of a criminal, and I am

sure you would never prevent a poor father of a family from gaining his living? Eh? Well, then, I have up stairs all the people who have come to see Bonnivard's dungeon. If you will promise me to remain quiet, and not attempt to escape— ."

The worthy Tartarin promised at once, and five minutes afterwards he saw his dungeon invaded by his old acquaintances of the Rigi-Kulm and the Tellsplatte: the ass Schwanthaler, the most inept Astier-Réhu, the member of the Jockey Club with his niece, all the Cook's tourists! Ashamed, and fearful of being recognised, the unhappy man hid behind the pillars, retiring and stealing away as they approached him, the tourists preceding the gaoler, who uttered his clap-trap in a melancholy tone: "This is where the unfortunate Bonnivard was imprisoned."

They advanced slowly, retarded by the disputes of the two *savants*, who were always quarrelling, ready to fly at each other, one waving his camp-stool, the other his *sac de voyage*, in fantastic attitudes, which the half-light magnified along the vaulted dungeon roof.

By the mere exigency of retreat, Tartarin found himself at last near the opening of the *oubliettes*— a black pit, open level with the ground, breathing an odour of many centuries, damp and cold. Alarmed, he stopped, crouched in a corner, his cap over his eyes; but the damp saltpetre of the walls affected him, and suddenly a loud sneeze, which made the tourists recoil, betrayed him!

"*Tiens*, Bonnivard!" exclaimed the fast little Parisienne in the Directoire hat, whom the member of the Jockey Club called his niece.

The Tarasconnais did not permit himself to show any signs of being disturbed.

"It is really very interesting, these *oubliettes!*" he remarked in the most natural tone in the world, as if he also was a mere visitor for pleasure to the dungeon. Then he mingled with the other tourists, who smiled on recognising the Alpinist of the Rigi-Kulm, the mainspring of that famous ball.

"*Hé! mossié! ballir, dantsir!*"

The comical outline of the little fairy Schwanthaler presented itself before him, ready to dance. Truly, he had a great mind to dance with her. Then, not knowing how to disembarrass himself of this excited little bit of a woman, he offered her his arm, and gallantly showed her his dungeon: the ring whereon the captive's chain had been riveted, the traces of his footsteps worn in the rock around the same pillar; and, never having heard Tartarin speak with such facility, the good lady never suspected that he who was walking with her was also a State prisoner—a victim to the injustice and the wickedness of men. Terrible, for instance, was the parting, when the unfortunate "Bonnivard," having led her to the door, took leave of her with the smile of a man of the world, saying:— "No, thank you, *vé!* I remain here a moment longer." She bowed, he bowed; and the gaoler, who was on the alert, locked and bolted the door, to the great astonishment of all.

What an insult! He was bathed in agonised perspiration as he listened to the exclamations of the departing visitors. Fortunately such torture as this could not be repeated that day. The bad weather would deter tourists. A terrible wind was blowing under the old planks; cries arose from the *oubliettes*, like the plaints of unburied bodies, and the ripple of the lake, dotted with the rain, beat against the walls to the edges of the embrasures whence the spray was dashed

"'Tiens! Bonnivard.'"

over the prisoner. At intervals the bell of a steamer, and the patter of its wheels, broke upon the reverie of poor Tartarin, while the evening descended grey and mournful on the dungeon, which seemed to grow larger.

How could this arrest be explained? How could his imprisonment be justified? Costecalde, perhaps—an electoral manœuvre at the last moment. Or had the Russian police been informed of his imprudent utterances, his proposal to Sonia, and had demanded his extradition? But then, why arrest the delegates? What could be alleged against these unfortunate men, whose alarm and despair he could picture, although they were not in the dungeon of Bonnivard, in these stony vaults, traversed at night by rats of enormous size, by crayfish, and silent spiders with hairy, uncanny feet.

Now you see what it is to have a good conscience. Notwithstanding the rats, the cold, and the spiders, the great Tartarin found, amid all the horrors of the State prison, haunted by the shades of martyrs, a rude sound sleep, with mouth open and hands clenched, as he had slept between the sky and the abysses in the hut of the Alpine Club. He thought he was still dreaming, when he heard his gaoler enter in the morning.

"Get up," said he; "the prefect of the district is here; he will question you;" and he added, with some respect: "You must be a famous criminal for the prefect to put himself out about you as he has done."

Criminal! No, but one may look like one after a night in a damp and dusty dungeon, without having any opportunity to make one's *toilette*, however quickly. And in the old stable of the castle, now transformed into a guard-house, embellished with muskets in racks—when Tartarin, after a reassuring glance at the Alpinists, who were seated amongst the *gendarmes*, appeared before the prefect of the district, he had the pleasure of feeling he was in the presence of a tidy, well-dressed magistrate, one who questioned him severely:

"You are named Maniloff, is not that so?—a Russian subject, an incendiary, a fugitive assassin from Siberia?"

"Never in my life! It is an error—a misprision!"

"Hold your tongue, or I will gag you," interrupted the captain.

The neat prefect continued: "Well, to cut short your denials—do you know this rope?"

His rope! *Coquin de sort!* His rope, with the iron fibre, made at Avignon. He bowed his head, to the stupefaction of the delegates, and replied, "I know it!"

"With this rope a man has been hanged in the Canton of Unterwald!"

Tartarin, trembling, swore that he knew nothing about that.

"We shall soon see." Then he introduced the Italian tenor, the detective, whom the Nihilists had hanged to the oak on the Brünig, but whom the woodcutters had miraculously delivered from death.

The spy looked at Tartarin: "That is not the man nor," he added, looking at the delegates, "are those the others. There has been a mistake here."

The prefect was furious: then, to Tartarin, "Well, then, what *have* you done?"

"That is just what I want to know, *vé!*" replied the President, with all the assurance of innocence.

After some explanations, the Alpinists of Tarascon, set at liberty, hurried away from Chillon, of which place no one has experienced the romantic and melancholy oppression more strongly than they. They stopped at the *pension* Müller, to get their luggage, the banner, and to pay the bill of the *déjeuner* they had not had time to eat: then they departed for Geneva by train. Rain was falling. Through the steaming windows they could see the names of the stations, Clarens, Vevay, Lausanne ; the red *chalets*, the gardens of rare shrubs—all lying under a damp veil, which dropped from the branches of the trees, the roofs of the houses, and the terraces of the hotels.

Installed in a corner of the long Swiss railway-carriage, two seats face to face, the Alpinists looked defeated and discomfited. Bravida, very bitter, complained of pain, and all the time kept asking Tartarin, with fierce irony: " Eh, *bé!* you haven't seen Bonnivard's dungeon, have you ? You wished to see it so much, too ! I believe you *have* seen it, after all, *qué ?* " Excourbaniès, voiceless for the first time in his life, gazed piteously at the lake, which the line skirted : " There is water enough, *Boudiou!* After this, I shall never take another bath as long as I live ! "

Upset by a shock from which he had not yet recovered, Pascalon, the banner between his knees, hid himself behind it, looking right and left, like a hare. And Tartarin ? Oh ! he ; always calm and dignified, he was improving his mind reading the papers from southern France, a packet of journals forwarded to the *pension* Müller, which had all copied from the *Forum* the narrative of his ascent—which he had dictated and enlarged—embellished by startling eulogies. All of a sudden, our hero uttered a cry—a loud cry which pervaded the carriage. All the travellers rose: they thought an accident had occurred. It was only that these words had caught Tartarin's eyes in the *Forum*—"Listen to this!" he cried to the Alpinists: "'It is reported that V. P. C. A. Costecalde, who has scarcely recovered from the jaundice which has afflicted him for some days, is about to leave here with a view to ascend Mont Blanc—to go higher up than Tartarin!' Ah! the bandit! He wants to destroy the effect of my Jungfrau! Well, wait a little; I will take the wind out of you and your mountain! Chamonix is only a few miles from Geneva—I will do Mont Blanc before him! Are you agreed, my boys?"

Bravida protested. *Outre!* He had had adventures enough. "Enough, and more than enough," growled Excourbaniès in a low tone, in his husky voice.

"And you, Pascalon?" asked Tartarin, gently.

The pupil bleated without raising his eyes: "Ma-as-ter!" He also denied him!

"Very well," said the hero, solemnly and sorrowfully. "Then I will go alone. I shall have all the honour. *Zou!* Give me the banner!"

XII

The Hôtel Baltet at Chamonix.—That smell of garlic!—Concerning the uses of the cord in Alpine excursions.—Shake hands!—A pupil of Schopenhauer's.—At the Grands-Mulets.—" Tartarin, I must speak to you."

THE clock of Chamonix was striking nine on a chilly, wet evening. All the streets were dark, all the houses shut up, except where occasionally the gas of the hotels blazed out and made the surroundings still more sombre in the vague reflection of the snow, a star of white under a night of sky.

At the Hôtel Baltet, one of the best and most frequented in the Alpine village, the numerous travellers and excursionists had dispersed by degrees, tired out by the fatigues of the day, so there remained in the grand *salon* only an English parson playing draughts with his wife, while his innumerable daughters in pinafore aprons were engaged in copying the notices for the next services; and seated, in front of the hearth, on which blazed a good fire of logs, a young Swede, hollow-cheeked and pale, who was regarding the fire with a mournful air while he drank *kirsch* and seltzer-water. Occasionally a belated tourist traversed the *salon* with soaked gaiters and glistening waterproof; went up to a big barometer hanging on the wall, tapped it, watched the mercury for the next day's weather, and turned away in consternation. Not a word, no other manifestation of life save the crackling of the fire, the dashing of the sleet against the windows, and the roaring of the Arve beneath the wooden bridge, a few yards from the hotel.

Suddenly the door of the *salon* was opened,

a silver-laced porter entered laden with valises and rugs, with four Alpinists, shivering, and bewildered by the sudden change from darkness and cold to light and warmth.

"*Boudiou!* what weather!"

"Something to eat, *zou!*"

"Warm the beds, *qué!*"

They all spoke together beneath their comforters and wraps and ear protectors, and no one knew which to listen to, until a short fat man, whom they called the President, imposed silence upon them by crying louder than all, in a commanding tone:

"Bring me the visitors' book first."

Then, turning the leaves with a benumbed hand, he read aloud the names of the travellers who, during the last eight days, had sojourned at the hotel. Doctor Schwanthaler and Frau—again! Astier-Réhu, of the French Academy! He turned over two or three pages, growing pale when he saw a name resembling that of which he was in search. Then at length, as he threw the book on the table with a triumphant laugh, the little man cut a caper—an extraordinary performance for such a fat little fellow—and cried : "He is not here, *vé !* he has not come ! He must come down here, at any rate. Bother Costecalde ! *lagadigadeou !* Quick with the soup, lads ! " And the worthy Tartarin, having bowed to the ladies, marched towards the *salle à manger*, followed by the delegates, hungry and noisy.

Eh? Yes; the delegates—all of them—Bravida himself amongst them ! Is it possible ! What would they have said yonder if they had gone home without Tartarin? Each one had felt the same. And in the moment of separation at the railway-station at Geneva the *buffet* was witness to a most heartrending scene of tears, embraces, and distressing farewells to the banner, — the result of which adieux was that the whole party crowded into the landau which the President had engaged to carry him to Chamonix. A superb route to which they firmly closed their eyes, swathed in wraps, snoring sonorously, without admiring the magnificent landscape which from Sallanches displayed itself through the rain: chasms, forests, foaming cascades, and, according to the windings of the valley, alternately visible or shrouded, the crest of Mont Blanc above the clouds. Fatigued by this kind of natural

beauty, the Tarasconnais only sought how to make up for the bad night they had passed under lock and key at Chillon. And now, once more, at the end of the long, deserted *salle à manger* of the Hôtel Baltet, while being served with the re-heated soup and removes of the *table d'hôte*, they ate ravenously, without speaking, only preoccupied in their desire to get to bed as quickly as possible.

Suddenly, Spiridion Excourbaniès, who had

been eating like a man in his sleep, rose up out of his place, and, sniffing the air, said:

"*Outre!* what a smell of garlic!"

"That's true, that is the smell," remarked Bravida; and all the party, aroused by this recall to their native land, this smell of the national dishes, which Tartarin had not breathed for a long while, turned in their chairs with gastronomic anxiety. The odour came from the other end of the *salle*, from a small room wherein was a traveller supping alone—no doubt a personage of importance, for every minute the cap of the *chef* was visible at the grating opening to the kitchen, to pass up a pile of little covered dishes, which were carried by the waitress to the little room.

"Some one from the South," murmured the gentle Pascalon; and the President, who had become pale at the idea of Costecalde, commanded:

"Go and see, Spiridion; you know what to say."

A loud burst of laughter arose from the room which the brave man had penetrated to by his chief's commands, whence he led in by the hand a long nosed individual with comic eyes, his *serviette* tucked under his chin, like the gastronomous horse.

"*Vé!* Bompard!"

"*Té!* The Impostor!"

"*Hé!* Adieu, Gonzague. *Comment te va?*"

"Pretty well, gentlemen; I am your most obedient," said the courier, shaking hands all round, and seating himself at the table with the Tarasconnais to partake with them a dish of *cèpes à l'ail*, prepared by Mère Baltet, who, as well as her husband, had a horror of the *table d'hôte* fare.

Whether it was the *fricot* or the delight of finding a resting place, the delightful Bompard was inexhaustibly imaginative. Immediately fatigue and the desire for sleep were dissipated; champagne was gulped in bumpers, and with moustaches glistening with bubbles, they laughed, screamed, gesticulated, embraced each other, full of effusiveness.

"I will not leave you any more," Bompard was saying. "My Peruvians have gone away. I am at liberty."

"At liberty! Then you can make the ascent of Mont Blanc with me to-morrow?"

"Ah, you are going to do Mont Blanc, *demain?*" replied Bompard without enthusiasm.

"Yes, I am going to put Costecalde's nose out of joint. When he comes, *uit!* No more Mont Blanc! You are with me, Gonzague?"

"I'm there, I'm there; if the weather suits. It is an ascent which is not always pleasant at this season."

"Ah! *vai* with your 'not pleasant!'" said the worthy Tartarin, winking with a meaning which Bompard, on his part, did not seem to understand.

"Let us have our coffee in the *salon.* We will consult with Père Baltet. He knows all about it. He is an old guide who has made the ascent twenty-seven times."

The delegates cried simultaneously:

"Twenty-seven times! *Boufre!*"

"Bompard is always exaggerating," said the P. C. A. severely, with a touch of envy.

In the *salon* they found the parson's family

still bent over the church notices, the father and mother nodding over their game of draughts, and the long Swede stirring his *kirsch* and seltzer with the same listless gesture. But the invasion of the Tarasconnais, brightened up by the champagne, gave some little entertainment, as we may imagine, to the young church-women. These charming young girls had never seen coffee taken with so much mimicry and so much rolling of eyes.

"Sugar, Tartarin?"

"Well, no, Commandant. You know that since I was in Africa——"

"True, pardon! *Të!* Here is M. Baltet."

"Sit down there, *qué*, M. Baltet."

"Long live M. Baltet! Ha! ha! *fen dé brut!*"

Surrounded and pressed upon by these people whom he had never seen in his life Père Baltet smiled calmly. A robust Savoyard, tall and broad-shouldered, his back rounded, his step slow, his thick and shaven face was lighted up by a pair of cunning eyes still youthful, contrasting with his baldness caused by a frost-bite one early morning on the snow-fields.

"These gentlemen wish to ascend Mont Blanc?" said he, gauging the Tarasconnais with a look at once humble and ironical. Tartarin was about to reply, but Bompard anticipated him:

"Is not the season rather advanced?"

"No," replied the old guide. "Here is a Swedish gentleman who will go up to-morrow; and I am expecting, at the end of the week, two American gentlemen to ascend also. One of them is blind."

"I know—I met him on the Guggi."

"Ah! monsieur has been to the Guggi?"

"Eight days ago, going up the Jungfrau."

There was a flutter among the Evangelical ladies, their plumes rustled, and they raised their heads to look at Tartarin, which action, for Englishwomen, who are great climbers, and experts in all sports, carried considerable authority. He had been up the Jungfrau!

"A good expedition," said Père Baltet, looking at the P. C. A. with astonishment; while Pascalon, alarmed by the ladies, blushed, and bleated:

"Ma - a - ster, tell them the — the *crevasse.*"

The President smiled: "Child!" But all the same he commenced his recital of his fall; first with a touch-and-go listless air, then he warmed up and illustrated the narrative with action, such as kicking at the end of the cord, over the chasm, appeals with stiffened hands, &c. The ladies shivered, devouring him with their cold English eyes—those eyes which open so widely and round.

In the silence that followed, the voice of Bompard rose loudly:

"Up on Chimborazo we do not tie ourselves to cross the *crevasses*."

The delegates looked at him. As a *Tarasconnade*, this beat everything! "Oh, that Bompard!" murmured Pascalon, with ingenuous admiration.

But Père Baltet, taking Chimborazo quite seriously, protested against the non-employment of the rope. According to his view, no ascent was possible on ice without ropes a good Manilla rope. At least, then, if one slipped, the others could hold him up.

"Supposing the rope does not break, Monsieur Baltet," said Tartarin, recalling the catastrophe on the Matterhorn.

But the hotel-keeper replied deliberately: "The rope did not break on the Matterhorn. The rear guide cut it with his axe."

As Tartarin became angry at this, he continued: "You must excuse me, monsieur; the guide was within his rights. He perceived the impossibility of holding the others, and he detached them to save the lives of himself, his son, and the traveller who had accompanied them. Had it not been for his determination, there would have been seven victims instead of four."

Then a discussion commenced. Tartarin maintained that, once attached to the line, it was a matter of honourable engagement to live or die together; and then, influenced by the presence of ladies, he rose to the occasion. He applied his words to facts, to people present. "Thus," said he, "when to-morrow, *té*, in attaching myself to Bompard, it would not be only a precaution that I would take, but an oath before Heaven and my fellow-men only to live with my companion, and to die rather than return without him, *coquin de sort!*"

" I accept the pledge for myself, as well as for you, Tartarin," exclaimed Bompard, from the other side of the round table.

This was an affecting moment.

The parson, as if electrified, rose and inflicted on our hero a pumping hand-grip, English fashion. His wife followed his example; while all his daughters continued to shake hands with a vigour which, properly applied, would have pumped water to the fifth story of the hotel. The delegates, I am bound to state, displayed less enthusiasm.

"Eh, *bé!* I am of M. Baltet's opinion," said Bravida. "In cases like these, it's every one for himself, *pardi!* and I can quite understand that stroke of the axe."

"You astonish me, Placide," said Tartarin, severely; then quite privately he added: "Hold, you miserable man—England is watching us!"

The old warrior, who decidedly had kept a store of bitterness in his heart since the excursion to Chillon, made a gesture which signified his contempt for "England," and perhaps he would have drawn upon himself a severe reprimand from the President, irritated by so much cynicism, when the young man with the melancholy mien, full of grog and sadness, introduced his bad French into the conversation. He also maintained that the guide was right to cut the rope—to put an end to the existence of four unhappy individuals still young, that is to say, condemned to live a certain time—to lay them to rest by one stroke—such an action was both noble and generous!

Tartarin at this exclaimed:

"How, young man! at your age, do you speak of life with this abandonment—this anger! What harm has existence done you?"

"Nothing; it merely bores me."

He was studying philosophy at Christiania, he had imbibed ideas from Schopenhauer and Hartmann, and found life gloomy, foolish, chaotic. Very near suicide, he had closed his books at his parents' urgent prayers, and had gone to travel; still meeting everywhere with the same *ennui*, the gloomy misery of the world. Tartarin and his friends appeared to him the only people contented to live whom he had hitherto met.

The good P. C. A. began to laugh. "The

race comes out there, young man. We are all the same at Tarascon, the country of *le Bon Dieu*. From morn till night we laugh, we sing, and the rest of the time we dance the *farandole*, like this—*té!*" Then he cut an *entrechat* with the grace and lightness of a great cockchafer spreading his wings.

But the delegates had not nerves of steel, or the indefatigable energy of their chief. Excourbaniès growled: "The *Présidain* is dancing, and it is close on midnight!"

Bravida rose in a rage: "Let us go to bed, *vé!* I shall not have any more of my sciatica there."

Tartarin consented, thinking of the ascent on the morrow; and the Tarasconnais went, candlestick in hand, up the wide granite staircase to their rooms, while the Père Baltet proceeded to busy himself about provisions and to engage guides and mules.

"*Té!* it snows!"

These were the first words which escaped Tartarin as he saw the frosted windows next morning, and perceived that the room was bathed in a white reflection; but when he hung up his little shaving-glass, he understood that he had been mistaken, and that Mont Blanc was glittering opposite in a bright sun and making all this light. He opened his

window to the breeze from the glacier, fresh and comforting, which carried to his ears all the tinkling of the cow-bells and the long bellowings of the shepherds' horns. Something strong and pastoral, which he had not breathed in Switzerland, filled the air.

Down stairs an assemblage of guides and porters awaited him. The Swede already had mounted, and, mingled with the spectators, who formed a circle, was the parson's family; all these brisk damsels, in morning *toilettes*, had come down to shake hands again with the hero who had haunted their dreams.

"A splendid morning! make haste!" cried the hotel-keeper, whose bald head shone in the sun like a pebble. Tartarin had need to hurry, for it was no light task to awake the delegates, who were to accompany him as far as the Pierre-Pointue, where the mule-path stops. Neither prayers nor expostulations could induce the Commandant to get up; with his nightcap down to his ears, and his nose against the wall, he contented himself with replying to the objurgations of the President by a cynical Tarasconnais proverb: "He who has a character for early rising may sleep till noon." As for Bompard, he kept repeating all the time: "Ah! get out with your Mont Blanc! what rubbish!" and he would not get up until formally commanded to do so by the President of the Alpine Club.

At length the party started, and crossed the little streets of Chamonix in a most imposing array—Pascalon in front, on a mule, the banner unfurled; and last, grave as a mandarin, amongst the guides and porters who surrounded his mule, Tartarin himself, a more curious Alpinist than ever, with a new pair of spectacles of smoked glass, and his famous rope made in Avignon, recovered we know at how great a price.

Stared at almost as much as the banner, he was delighted beneath that mask of importance, pleased with the picturesqueness of the streets of the Savoyard village, so different from the Swiss village—too clean, too varnished, like a new toy, the bazaar *chalet*—the contrast of these buildings scarcely above ground, in which the stable occupies nearly all the space, with the large, sumptuous hotels, five stories high, whose glaring signs strike one equally as do the silver-banded cap of a porter, the black suit and the pumps of the *maître d'hôtel*, in the midst of the Savoyard costumes, the caps, the fustian, and the coalheavers' hats with large flaps. On the *place* are some unhorsed vehicles, travelling-carriages side by side with dung-carts; a drove of pigs basking in the sun before the post-office, whence exits an Englishman with his packet of letters and his *Times*, which he reads as he walks, before opening his correspondence. The cavalcade traversed all this, accompanied by the whinnying of the mules, the war-cry of Excourbaniès, to whom the sun has restored the use of his "gong," the pastoral carillon on the slopes, and the roaring of the glacier-torrent—quite white, shining as if it were carrying with it sun and snow.

At the end of the village, Bompard approached his mule to that of the President, and said to him, as he rolled his extraordinary eyes: "Tartar*in*, I must speak to you!"

"By and by," said the P. C. A., who was deep in a philosophic discussion with the young Swede, from whom he was endeavouring to drive out the black pessimism by means of the marvellous spectacle which surrounded them—the pastures with their wide zones of light and shade, those forests of dark green crested with the whiteness of the glittering *névé*.

After two attempts to approach Tartarin,

Bompard gave up the idea perforce. After crossing the Arve by a little bridge, the caravan found itself on one of those narrow pathways

which wind through the pine-woods, on which the mules, one by one, shave all the turns of the track above the abysses, and the Tarasconnais had quite enough to do to keep their equilibrium by the aid of " *Allons!* " " *Douce-*

main!" "*Outre!*" by which they managed their animals.

At the hut on the Pierre-Pointue, in which Pascalon and Excourbaniès were to await the return of the climbers, Tartarin, very much occupied in ordering breakfast and in looking after the guides and porters, turned still a deaf ear to Bompard. But it was a curious thing, which no one remarked until later, that notwithstanding the fine weather and the good wine, the pure air, 6000 feet above the sea, the *déjeuner* was melancholy. While the guides were laughing and joking on their side, the Tarasconnais were silent, occupied solely with the table, and the only noise being the clinking of glasses and the rattling of dishes on the wooden board. Was it the presence of the mournful Swede, or the anxiety visible in the face of Gonzague, or some presentiment? The party continued the journey, as melancholy as a regiment without music, towards the glacier Des Bossons where the real ascent begins.

When putting his foot on the ice, Tartarin could not help smiling at the recollection of the Guggi, and his patent *crampons*. What a contrast between the neophyte he there had been, and the first-class Alpine climber he felt he had become! Firm on his heavy boots, which the porter at the hotel had spiked with four big nails, expert in the use of his axe, he scarcely required the assistance of the guides, and less to sustain himself than to have the route indicated. The smoked glasses tempered the glare of the glacier, which a recent avalanche had powdered with fresh snow, where the little "lakes" of sea-green tint appeared here and there slippery and treacherous; and quite calm, assured by experience that there was no danger whatever, Tartarin strode alongside the smooth shining *crevasses*, infinitely deep, passing amidst *séracs*, only careful to place his feet behind the Swedish student, an intrepid climber, whose silver-buckled gaiters continued to step out short and clean, and at the same distance from the point of his alpenstock, which seemed a third limb. Their philosophical discussion continued in spite of the difficulties of the route, and people could hear in the frozen air a sonorous sound as of a river, a hearty, familiar voice puffing out, "You know me, Otto!"

Bompard, all this time, was experiencing many adventures. Firmly convinced till that morning that Tartarin would never proceed with his boast, and that he (Bompard) would never do Mont Blanc any more than he had done the Jungfrau, the unhappy courier was clothed in his ordinary costume, without nailing his boots, nor even utilising his famous invention for shoeing the feet of soldiers; he had no alpenstock either—the mountaineers of Chimborazo did not require them! Armed only with the cane which suited well his round hat and his ulster, the approach to the glacier terrified him, for, notwithstanding all his tales, the others knew pretty well that the Impostor had never made an ascent. He consoled himself, however, when he perceived from the *moraine* how well Tartarin got on on the ice, and he decided to follow him up to the Grands-Mulets, where they intended to pass the night. At the first step, he fell on his back, and the second time on his hands

"The ulster swept the ice like the coat of a white bear."

and knees. "No, no," he said to the guide who offered to assist him, "it is done on purpose. The American fashion, *vé!* as at Chimborazo!" This attitude seemed to him comfortable, so he retained it, advancing on all fours, his hat on the back of his head, and his ulster training behind him like the coat of a white bear; very calm withal, and telling those near him how, amid the Cordilleras of the Andes, he had climbed in this fashion a mountain 30,000 feet high. He did not say how long it took him, by the by, but it must have been a very considerable time, judging by the stage up to the Grands-Mulets, where he arrived an hour after Tartarin, dripping with snow, while his hands were half-frozen under his worsted, knitted gloves.

Compared with the hut on the Guggi, the cabin erected by the commune of Chamonix at the Grands-Mulets, is truly comfortable. When Bompard came into the kitchen, in which a bright wood fire was burning, he found Tartarin and the Swede drying their boots, while the hut-keeper, an old shrivelled-up individual, with long white hair falling in curls, was exhibiting to them the treasures of his little museum.

Somewhat sad was this museum of *souvenirs* of catastrophes on Mont Blanc for a space of forty years, during which period the old man had kept the inn (hut); and, while taking the objects from their cases, he told their lamentable history. That morsel of cloth, those waistcoat-buttons, preserved the memory of a Russian *savant*, precipitated by a whirlwind over the glacier of the Brenva. Those teeth were the remains of a guide of the famous party of eleven travellers and porters who disappeared in a snow-storm. In the light of the dying day, and the pale reflection of the *névé* against the glass, the surroundings of these relics, the monotonous recital of them had something painful in them, so much so that the old man's voice trembled in the pathetic parts, and he was even moved to tears in displaying the green veil of an English lady who perished in an avalanche in 1827.

Tartarin had only to compare dates to convince himself that at that time the Company was not in existence to arrange non-dangerous ascents, yet this *vero* Savoyard touched him, and he went to the door for a little fresh air.

Night came on, and shrouded the depths. The Bossons stood out livid, and seemed very near, while Mont Blanc rose high, still caressed by the ruddy beams of the setting sun. The Southern traveller was recovering himself at the sight of this smile of Nature, when the shade of Bompard came behind him.

"Ah! 'tis you, Gonzague? you see I am enjoying the pure air. That old man rather made me feel foolish with his reminiscences."

"Tartar*ein*," said Bompard, catching hold of his companion's arm forcibly, "I hope

that you have had enough of this, and that you are going to end this ridiculous expedition here."

The great man opened his eyes with some anxiety in them:

"What *are* you chattering about?"

Then Bompard drew a picture of the

thousand terrible deaths which menaced them
the *crevasses*, the avalanches, the storms,
the whirlwinds of snow!

Tartarin interrupted him:

"Ah! *vaï*, you joker! And the Company? Is not Mont Blanc managed in the same manner as the rest?"

"Managed! the Company!" exclaimed Bompard, who remembered nothing of his *Tarasconnade;* and when the other repeated it word for word--the Swiss Society, the "farming" out of the mountains, the claptrap *crevasses*, &c.,—the former manager began to laugh:

"What! did you believe all that? Why, it was only a *galéjade*. Between people of Tarascon, of course -- we know that what we say is —is— --"

"Then the Jungfrau *was not prepared?*" said Tartarin, very much excited.

"By no means."

"And if the rope had broken?"

"Ah! my poor friend!"

The hero shut his eyes, pale with the horrifying retrospection, and for a moment he did not speak. This landscape, like a polar cataclysm—cold, sombre, undulated, broken; those lamentations of the old inn-keeper still ringing in his ears. "*Outre!* What made you tell me so?" Then, suddenly, he thought of the *geusses* at Tarascon, of the banner which he had flung out above, and he said to himself that, with good guides, a companion of such proved experience as Bompard——well, he had accomplished the Jungfrau—why not attempt Mont Blanc?

Then, placing his large hand on the shoulder of his friend, he said in a manly voice:

"Listen, Gonzague!"

XIII

The Catastrophe.

IN a dark night, a moonless darkness, no stars, no visible sky, on the white quivering surface of an immense snow slope, is unrolled a long rope, to which some fearful shadows, and all small ones, are attached in single file, preceded a hundred yards in advance by a lantern, with a red disk, almost at the level of the ground. Blows of an ice-axe ring in the hard snow, the rattling of the detached lumps of ice alone break the silence of the snow-field, as the steps are cut for the travellers; then from time to time a cry, a stifled complaint, the fall of a body on the ice, and suddenly a stout voice, which answers from the end of the rope, "Go gently, Gonzague!" For the poor Bompard has made up his mind to follow his friend Tartarin to the summit of Mont Blanc. Since two o'clock in the morning—it is now four by the President's repeater—the unhappy courier has been advancing, groping in the dark, a very convict on the chain, dragged forward, pushed up, swaying, and stumbling; compelled to restrain the varied exclamations which his mishaps would have wrung from him; for the avalanche threatened on all sides, the least disturbance—a little vibration of the clear air—would determine the fall of the snow or the ice. To suffer in silence—what a torture for a man of Tarascon!

But the party had halted: Tartarin asked why. A discussion was heard in a low voice, in animated whispers: "It is your companion who does not wish to advance any farther," said the Swede. The order of march was changed, the human chaplet extended, turned back on itself, and the party found itself on the edge of an enormous *crevasse*, one which mountaineers call a "*roture.*" The previous ones had been crossed by means of a ladder placed across them, over which the climbers crawled on hands and knees: in this case, the *crevasse* was much too wide, and the other lip raised itself eighty to a hundred feet high. The descent had to be made to the bottom of the hole, which narrowed very much, and then the ascent on the opposite side in like manner. But Bompard obstinately declined.

Leaning over the chasm, which the darkness caused to appear unfathomable, he watched the guides making the necessary preparations by the light of the lantern. Tartarin, who was himself by no means easy in his mind, gave himself courage by exhorting his friend: "Come, Gonzague, *zou!*" and then, in a lower tone, he appealed to his honour; he invoked Tarascon, the banner, and the Alpine Club.

"Ah! *vaï*, the Club—I no longer belong to it," he replied, cynically.

Then Tartarin explained to him where to put his feet, than which nothing could be more easy.

"Yes, for you perhaps, but not for me!"

"Why not? You say you have been in the habit——"

"*Bé!* yes, certainly the habit, but of what? I have so many habits. The habit of smoking or sleeping——"

"Particularly of lying!" interrupted the President.

"Of exaggerating, if you will," replied Bompard, without moving a muscle.

However, after much hesitation, the threat to leave him all alone decided him in descending slowly and carefully this terrible Jacob's ladder. To ascend was more difficult, as the opposite wall is as slippery and smooth as marble, and higher than the Réné Tower at Tarascon. From below, the guide's lamp looked a very glow-worm. It was necessary to make up one's mind, nevertheless. The snow under foot was not solid; the dropping of a spring, and running water, were making a large fissure, which the men could guess at better than they could see, at the foot of the ice-wall, and which sent up a cold breath from the abyss.

"Go gently, Gonzague, for fear of falling!"

This phrase, which Tartarin enunciated in an almost supplicatory manner, lent a solemn significance to the respective positions of the ascensionists, hanging now by hands and feet, one over the other, tied by a rope, and by the similarity of their movements; so that the fall or the awkwardness of one would put all in danger. And what danger, *coquin de sort!* It was quite enough to listen to the falling and the disintegration of the *débris* of the iceblocks, and the echo of the fall in the *crevasses* and the unknown depths, to imagine what a monster's throat you would fall into should you happen to make a false step.

But what happened? The long Swede, who immediately preceded Tartarin, stopped, and touched the cap of the P. C. A. with his iron-shod heel. The guides kept crying, "*En avant!*" and the President, "*Avancez donc, jeune homme.*" But he never stirred. Hanging to his full length, and holding with a negligent hand, the Swede looked down, as the breaking day lightened his fair beard, and illumined the curious expression of his dilated eyes, while he made a sign to Tartarin:

"What a fall, eh, if one let go!"

"*Outre!* I believe you. You would carry us all down with you. Go on!"

The other continued, without moving:

"A splendid opportunity to have done with life, to re-enter nothingness through the bowels of the earth, to roll from *crevasse* to *crevasse*, like this piece of ice I kick away." As he spoke, he bent over, fearfully, to watch the piece he had detached, which bounded apparently going on for ever—through the night.

"Unhappy man, take care!" exclaimed Tartarin, pale from fear; and, desperately clinging to the wall, he resumed his argument of the day before, concerning the advantages of existence: "It is good—at your age a fine fellow like you. You have never known what love is, *qué?*"

No; the Swede knew nothing of it. Ideal love is the falsehood of poets; the other, a want which he had never experienced.

"*Bé oui! bé oui!* It is true that the poets are something Tarasconic. They very often say more than they need; but, at any rate, the *femellan*—as they call women in our district—is *gentil.* Then one has children—pretty little things, who resemble one!"

"Ah! yes, the children—a source of misery! Since I was born, my mother has not ceased to weep!"

"Listen, Otto; you know me, my good friend."

Then with all the valorous expansion of his soul, Tartarin set about to reanimate, to rub back to life, this victim of Schopenhauer and Hartmann; two punchinellos, who ought to be banished as a punishment for all the evil they have done to young men.

Let us remember, during this philosophic discussion, the high wall of ice—cold, sea-green, glistening with a pale yellow light—and the human bodies spotted on its surface, with the sinister gurglings which kept ascending from the abyss; the oaths of the guides, and their threats to detach themselves and leave the tourists, were all accompaniments.

At length, Tartarin, perceiving that no reasoning could convince this madman, or dissipate his infatuation, suggested to him the idea of throwing himself from the extreme summit of Mont Blanc. That would really be worth the trouble! A splendid finish in space. But to die here, at the bottom of a cave! Ah! *vaï*, what *foutaise!* He put into the word so much persuasiveness of accent and such conviction that the Swede

permitted himself to yield, and then at length, one by one, they gained the summit of this terrible *roture*.

They untied themselves, and waited to drink and eat a little. Day was breaking—a cold pallid day—upon a magnificent amphitheatre of peaks and pinnacles, dominated by Mont Blanc, still 4500 feet above. The guides gesticulated and conversed apart, with many nods of their heads. On the white ground the round-backed, heavy men looked like marmots. Bompard and Tartarin were restless and anxious, and left the Swede to eat by himself, while they came up to the group just as the chief guide was saying:

"When he smokes his pipe we must only say, 'No.'"

"Who is smoking his pipe?" asked Tartarin.

"*Le Mont Blanc, monsieur.* Look!"

The man indicated, at the highest peak, a white smoke which was blowing towards Italy.

"Well, my good friend, and when Mont Blanc smokes his pipe what does it portend?"

"It means, monsieur, that a storm is raging at the summit—a snow-storm—which will be upon us ere long. And, *dame!* it is dangerous!"

"Let us return," said Bompard, turning green; and Tartarin added:

"Yes, yes, certainly; no foolish swagger!"

But the Swede came up and struck in. He had paid to go up Mont Blanc, and nothing would prevent him from going. He would ascend alone if no one would accompany him. "Cowards! cowards!" he added, turning to the guides; and he repeated the insult in the same ghostly voice with which he had been urging himself to suicide just before.

"You will very soon see whether we are cowards! Attach yourselves! *En route!*" exclaimed the chief guide. This time it was Bompard who protested energetically. He had had enough; he wished that they would take him back. Tartarin seconded him strongly:

"You see quite well that this young man is mad!" he exclaimed, indicating the Swede, who had already strode off amid the wisps of snow which the wind was throwing in all directions. But nothing would stop these men, who had been called "cowards." The marmots had been aroused, and Tartarin could not obtain a guide to lead him and Bompard to the Grands-Mulets. However, the direction was easy. Three hours' walking, allowing a *détour* of twenty minutes to "turn" the great *roture*, if they were afraid to pass it alone.

"*Outre!* yes, we are afraid," said Bompard, without any shame; and the two parties separated.

Now the Tarasconnais were alone. They advanced with precaution over the desert of snow, attached to the same cord, Tartarin in advance, prodding with his alpenstock gravely, imbued with the responsibility which devolved upon him, searching for some comfort.

"Courage and coolness! We shall extricate ourselves!" he said every instant to Bompard. Thus the officer in battle chases away the fear he feels by brandishing his sword and crying out to his men:

"*En avant!* all bullets do not kill!"

At length, behold our travellers at the edge of the horrible *crevasse*. Thence there were no grave obstacles; but the wind blew, and blinded them with little snowstorms. Advance became impossible without danger of losing their way.

"Let us wait here a moment," said Tartarin. A gigantic *sérac* gave them shelter at its base; they crept in, stretched over them the doubled waterproof of the President, and emptied the rum-flask, the only provision which had been left them by the guides. They

thus obtained a little heat and comfort, while the sound of the step-cutting above them, growing feebler and feebler, gave them an idea of the progress of the expedition. The sound echoed in the heart of the President like a regret for not having ascended to the summit of Mont Blanc.

"Who will know that?" remarked Bompard, cynically. "The porters have retained the banner, and the people at Chamonix will think it is you."

"You are right; the honour of Tarascon is safe," concluded Tartarin, in a tone of conviction.

But the elements became furious—the *bise* in a storm, the snow in masses. The two friends remained silent, haunted by sinister thoughts: they recalled the museum of the old man at the Mulets, his lamentable narratives, the tale of the American tourist, who was found petrified with cold and hunger, holding in his frozen hand a note-book, in which his last thoughts were inscribed till the last convulsion which shook the pencil and caused his signature to swerve.

"Have *you* a note-book, Gonzague?"

And the other, who understood without any explanation, replied:

"Ah! *vaï*, a note-book! Do you think I am going to let myself die like that American? *Vite!* let us be off; come away."

"Impossible! At the first step we shall be

carried away like straws, and dashed into some chasm!"

"But then we must shout; the inn is not far from here." And Bompard, on his knees, his head protruding from the *sérac* in the attitude of a cow lowing, shouted: "Help! Help!"

"*Aux armes!*" cried Tartarin in his turn, in his most sonorous voice, which the grotto echoed like thunder.

Bompard seized him by the arm: "Miserable man, the *sérac!*" Positively the whole block trembled; another breath, and the mass of accumulated ice-blocks would fall upon them. They remained frozen, motionless, wrapped in a terrible silence, which was soon broken by a distant rumbling, which came nearer and nearer, increased, spread over the horizon, and finally died away underground in the gulfs of the ice.

"Poor fellows!" murmured Tartarin, thinking of the Swede and his guides, carried away by the avalanche, no doubt. Bompard shook his head: "We shall scarcely fare better next time," he said. In fact, their situation had become very critical; they did not dare to move in their ice-grotto, nor could they venture out in the storm.

To complete their terror of mind, from the valley now arose the baying of a dog—a death-wail. Suddenly, Tartarin, with staring eyes and trembling lips, seized the hands of his companion, and, looking at him kindly, said:

"Forgive me, Gonzague; yes, yes, forgive me. I have often been unkind to you. I treated you as a liar——"

"Ah! *vaï*, what does that matter?"

"I have as little right as any one to do so, for I have told many lies in my life, and at this supreme hour I feel the necessity to confess—to relieve my feelings—to publicly avow my impostures!"

"Impostures! You?"

"Listen to me, friend; in the first place, I never killed that lion!"

"That does not surprise me at all," replied Bompard, quickly. "But why should you worry yourself about so little? It is the sun which causes it; we are born with the lying faculty. *Vé!* myself—have I ever told the truth since I came into the world? As soon as I open my mouth, my Southern blood ascends. The people of whom I speak — well, I do not know them! The countries? I have never been in them! and all this makes such a tissue of invention that I can't even unravel it myself!"

"It is imagination, *pechère!*" sighed Tartarin. "We are liars in imagination!"

"And such lies have never done any one any harm; while an envious person, such a one as Costecalde——"

"Let us not speak of the wretch!" interrupted the P. C. A., seized with sudden rage. "*Coquin de bon sort!* It is, all the same, a little annoying— –" He suddenly stopped at a gesture from Bompard. "Ah! yes, the *sérac*," and lowering his voice, forced to swallow his anger, poor Tartarin continued his imprecations in a low voice, with an enormous and comical disarticulation of his mouth: "It is rather annoying to die in the flower of one's age by the fault of a scoundrel who at this moment is taking his *demi-tasse* comfortably in the *Tour de ville!*"

But while he was fulminating, the sky was clearing by degrees. The snow ceased, the wind dropped, blue rifts appeared above the grey of the clouds. Quick—away! They had re-tied themselves, when Tartarin, who had taken the lead as before, turned round and said, finger on his mouth:

"You know, Gonzague, all that has been said is quite between ourselves."

"*Tè, pardi!*"

Full of ardour, they resumed their way, plunging up to their knees into the newly-fallen snow, which had obliterated all traces of the party's ascent, so Tartarin consulted his compass every moment. But this Tarascon compass, accustomed to a hot climate, had been frozen since its arrival in Switzerland. The needle played puss-in the-corner, agitated and trembling; so the men proceeded straight before them, expecting to see suddenly the black rocks of the Grands-Mulets, calm amongst the uniform whiteness, amid the peaks, needles, and towers, which surrounded them; which dazzled and alarmed them too, for dangerous *crevasses* might be hidden under their feet.

"Coolness, Gonzague, coolness!"

"That is just what I require," replied Bompard lamentably. Then he groaned: "Oh, my foot,—oh, my leg—we are lost: we never shall get home again!"

They walked for two hours towards the middle of a snow-slope very hard to climb. Then Bompard cried, alarmed:

"Tartar*éin*, this ascends!"

"Eh! I can see that very well," replied the President, who seemed disturbed.

"But in my opinion we ought to be going down!"

"*Bé!* yes; but what do you want me to

do? If we keep ascending, we may get down the other side!"

That was descending indeed, and terribly, by a succession of *névés*, almost pointed glaciers, and beyond all this dangerous expanse of white a hut was perceived perched on a rock at a depth that seemed inaccessible. It would be a refuge for the night if they could reach it, as they had lost the direction of the Grands-Mulets—but at the cost of what efforts, what perils, perhaps!

"Whatever you do, don't let me go, Gonzague!"

"Neither you me, Tartarin!"

They exchanged these assurances without seeing each other, being separated by an *arête* behind which Tartarin had disappeared, the one advancing to ascend, the other to descend, slowly and in fear. They said no more, concentrating all their strength for fear of a false step, or a slip. Suddenly, when he was not more than a yard from the crest, Bompard heard a fearful cry from his companion. At the same time, he felt the rope give way with violence, and with an

"*Outre!*"
"*Boufre!*"

irregular severance. He endeavoured to resist, to fix himself, in order to sustain his companion over the abyss. But the rope was old, no doubt, for at last it snapped suddenly under the strain.

"*Outre!*"

"*Boufre!*"

These two cries arose, wild and despairing, in the silence and the solitude. Then succeeded a terrible calm—the calmness of death, which nothing could trouble more, in the vastness of the immaculate snows!

Towards evening, a man vaguely resembling Bompard—a spectre, dishevelled, wounded, in profuse perspiration reached the *auberge* of the Grands-Mulets, where they rubbed him, warmed him, and put him to bed, ere he could pronounce the words—almost choked with tears, and interrupted by the clenching of his hands towards heaven: "Tartarin—lost—rope broke!" At length they understood the great disaster which had happened.

While the old inn-keeper was lamenting, and

adding a new chapter to his accidents on the mountain, pending the arrival of new relics, the Swede and his guides, who had returned from their expedition, set out in search of the unfortunate Tartarin, with ropes, ladders, and all the apparatus, alas! without effect. Bompard remained as if stupefied, and was unable to furnish any precise information as to the place where the accident took place. They only found on the Dôme du Goûter an end of rope which remained in a fissure of the ice. But, curiously enough, this rope was cut as with a sharp instrument, so as to leave two ends. The newspapers of Chambéry gave a *facsimile* of it. At length, after eight days' searching, conscientiously undertaken, when every one was convinced that the poor *Présidain* was lost without hope of recovery, the delegates, despairing, returned to Tarascon, carrying Bompard with them—for his skull showed traces of a terrible fall.

"Don't talk to me about it," he would say, whenever the accident was mentioned to him. "Never speak to me on the subject!"

Decidedly, Mont Blanc now reckoned one more victim! And what a victim!

XIV

Epilogue.

A MORE impressive place than Tarascon cannot be found under the sun. Sometimes, in high *fête*, on Sundays, when all the town is out of doors—the drums beating, the *Cours* festive and noisy, dotted with green and red costumes, and on the great party-coloured posters the announcements of the wrestling matches for men and youths, and the bull-rings—it is enough for a practical joker to call out "Mad dog!" or "Escaped bull!" for the whole population to run in-doors, bolt themselves in, the outside Venetian blinds clattering as if in a storm, and lo! there is Tarascon deserted, silent, not a cat visible, not a sound audible, even the grasshoppers themselves are cowering and attentive listeners.

Such was the appearance of Tarascon on this particular morning, when it was neither *fête* day nor Sunday. The shops were closed, the houses shut up, squares and courts seemingly larger in the solitude. "*Vasta silentio*," said Tacitus, when describing Rome on the occasion of the funeral of Germanicus; and the comparison of Rome in mourning would apply so much better to Tarascon, inasmuch as a funeral service was being performed for the soul of Tartarin at that time in the metropolitan church, where the population *en masse* was weeping for its hero, its divinity, its invincible one with the double muscles, who lay amid the glaciers of Mont Blanc.

Now, while the tolling bell was showering its sad notes upon the deserted streets, Mlle. Tournatoire, the Doctor's sister, who in consequence of her delicate health always remained in-doors, shivering in her great arm-chair by the window, was looking out as she listened to the bells. The Tournatoires' house was on the Avignon road, almost opposite to Tartarin's house, and the sight of that illustrious domicile, to which the proprietor would never return, the garden-gate for ever closed—all, even to the boot-brushing boxes of the two little Savoyards by the door, made the heart of the poor lady swell; a secret passion for the hero having devoured her for more than thirty years! O mysteries of the heart of an old maid! It had been her happiness to see him pass at his regular time, and to say, "Where are you going?" to watch the alterations in his costume, whether he dressed in his Alpine habiliments or in the green coat! Now, she would never see him more! And even the consolation of praying for him with the other ladies of the town was denied to her.

Suddenly, the long, white cheeks of Mlle. Tournatoire coloured slightly; her pale eyes, rimmed with rose-colour, dilated considerably;

while her thin hand, with its prominent wrinkles, formed the sign of the cross. He! 'twas he! sidling along the wall at the other side of the street. At first she was

under the impression that she had seen an apparition. No, it was Tartarin himself in flesh and blood; only pale, piteous-looking, shabby; sidling along the wall like a poor man or a thief. But to explain his furtive presence at Tarascon we must return to Mont Blanc, to the Dôme du Goûter, at the precise

"On that triumphal road... at the head of his cap-shooters."

time when the two friends found themselves one on each side of the Dôme, Bompard feeling the rope which attached him to his friend suddenly stretched, as if by the falling of a body!

In fact, the rope had caught between two masses of ice; and Tartarin, feeling the same shock, also believed that his companion had fallen, and would drag him with him! So, in that supreme moment—how am I to tell it? *mon Dieu!*—in the agony of fear, both men, forgetting the solemn oath at the Hôtel Baltet, by a simultaneous movement and the same instinctive gesture, cut the rope! Bompard with his hunting-knife, and Tartarin with his ice-axe; then, overwhelmed by their crime, both convinced that they had sacrificed their friend, fled in opposite directions!

When the spectre of Bompard appeared at the Grands-Mulets, that of Tartarin reached the canteen of d'Avesailles. How, by what miracle, after so many falls and *glissades?* Mont Blanc alone can tell; for the poor P. C. A. remained two days in complete insensibility, incapable of uttering the slightest sound. As soon as he was fit, he came down to Courmayeur, the Italian Chamonix. At the hotel he heard nothing but the report of the melancholy catastrophe on Mont Blanc, quite a pendant to that on the Cervin: another Alpine climber killed in consequence of the fracture of the rope.

In the conviction which he experienced concerning Bompard, Tartarin, torn by remorse, did not dare to rejoin the delegates nor return home. He anticipated in all eyes and on every lip: "Cain, where is thy brother?" However, the want of funds, the condition of his wardrobe, the cold of September, which emptied the hotels, compelled him to proceed homewards. After all, no one had seen him commit the crime. Nothing need prevent him from inventing no matter what tale; and, the distractions of the journey assisting, he commenced to pull himself together again. But as he approached Tarascon, when he saw the fine lines of the *Alpines* standing forth against the blue sky, all the shame, remorse, and fear of being brought to justice seized upon him again; and, to avoid the scandal of an arrival on the railway-station, he quitted the train at the last station before the town was reached.

Ah! on this fine Tarascon road, all white and crackling with dust, without any other shade than the posts and the telegraph-wires, on this triumphal way where so many times he had marched at the head of his Alpinists or his cap-shooters, who would have recognised him, the valiant, the spruce, under those torn and dirty clothes, with that defiant, restless gaze watching the *gendarmes?* The day was very warm though the season was declining, and the water-melon which he purchased from a hawker, and ate in the shade of the cart, seemed to him delicious, while the peasant declaimed against the want of custom in Tarascon that morning, "because a mass for the dead was being said, for a person found away there in a hole in the mountains! *Tè!* the bells were tolling—they could hear them where they stood!"

There was no longer room for doubt: it was for Bompard, who had fallen, that this lugubrious carillon of death was carried by the wind over the lonely surrounding districts.

What an accompaniment to the return of a great man to his native place!

One minute, the door of the little garden was suddenly opened and shut. Tartarin found himself again at home—he saw the narrow paths bordered with trim box edging, and quite tidy; the basin, the fountain, the gold-fish darting away as the sand crackled under his feet, and the giant baobab in the flower-pot — a touching appearance of comfort ; the warmth of his home as a domestic rabbit enveloped him like a cloak of safety after all his dangers and adventures. But the bells—the cursèd bells—redoubled their clangour, and their deep notes crushed into his heart anew. They kept saying to him in funereal tones : " Cain, where is thy brother ? Tartarin, what hast thou done with Bompard ? " Then, without having the courage to move, he seated himself on the sunny edge of the little basin, and remained there exhausted and pensive, to the great disturbance of the gold-fish.

The bells have ceased. The church porch, lately so animated, is given up to the beggar-woman seated there as motionless as the stone saints. The religious ceremony is over, all Tarascon has proceeded to the Alpine Club, where in solemn session Bompard is about to give an account of the catastrophe, and to detail the incidents connected with the last moments of the President. Besides the members, many privileged persons, military, clerical, noble, and mercantile, had taken their places in the conference hall, of which the large open windows permitted the band stationed below on the steps, to mingle some heroic chords with the discourses of these gentlemen. An enormous crowd pressed around the musicians, standing on tip-toe and stretching their necks in the attempt to catch some fragments of the discourse; but the windows were too high up, and they could obtain no impressions as to what was passing within, except from two or three youngsters perched in a tree hard by, who threw scraps of information as one throws nuts or cherries from the top of a tree.

"*Vé* Costecalde, who is trying to make himself weep! Ah! the blackguard, he holds the chair at present. And poor Bézuquet, how he blows his nose, how red his eyes are! *Té!* they have put *crêpe* on the banner. And Bompard is coming to the table with the three delegates. He puts something on the desk. He speaks now. That must be beautiful! Look, how the tears are falling!"

As a matter of fact, the tenderness became

"And the water-melon he bought from a hawker seemed to him delicious."

general as Bompard advanced in his fantastic recital. Ah! memory came back to him again also imagination! After relating how he and his illustrious companions got to the

summit of Mont Blanc, without guides, for all had refused to follow them, being alarmed by the bad weather, and how they alone, with the banner displayed, for five minutes stood upon the highest peak in Europe, he proceeded to recount —and with what emotion!—

the perilous descent and the fall—Tartarin rolling to the bottom of a *crevasse*, and he, Bompard, attaching himself to a rope two hundred feet in length, had explored the hideous chasm throughout its whole length!

"More than twenty times, gentlemen—what do I say?—more than ninety times did I sound that abyss of ice without being able to reach our poor *Présidain*, whose fall, nevertheless, I could trace in consequence of some *débris* left in the crevices of the ice."

As he spoke, he laid on the table a fragment of a jaw-bone, some hairs from a beard, a piece of a waistcoat, and a buckle from a pair of braces—one would have declared they came from the relic-cases at the Grands-Mulets!

In face of this testimony, the transports of grief could no longer be restrained; even the hardest hearts, the partisans of Costecalde and the gravest persons—Cambalalette the notary, Doctor Tournatoire—shed, most effectively, some tears as large as decanter stoppers. The ladies present uttered piercing cries, which dominated even the sobbing howls of

Excourbaniès and the bleatings of Pascalon, while the funeral march, played by the band, accompanied all with a slow and lugubrious bass.

Then, when he perceived the emotion and distress his peroration had caused, Bompard ended his speech with a fine gesture of pity towards the remains, as conclusive evidence: "'There, dear friends and fellow-citizens, is all I could discover of our illustrious and well-beloved President. The remains the glacier will render up to us — in forty years!"

He was about to explain, for the benefit of ignorant people, the recent discovery of the regular progress of glaciers; but the creaking of the little door at the end interrupted him —some one was coming in. Tartarin, paler than a spirit of Hume's raising, stood before the speaker!

" *Vé!* Tartarin!"

" *Té!* Gonzague!"

And this race is so singular, so *facile*, in the matter of improbable stories, audacious falsehoods and quick refutations, that the arrival of the great man, whose fragments still lay on the table, did not create any particular astonishment throughout the hall.

"It is a misapprehension, *allons!*" said Tartarin, very much relieved radiant with

his hand on the shoulder of the man he had believed he had killed. "I did the Mont Blanc on two sides—ascended on one, descended on the other—and this quite accounts for my disappearance."

He did not confess that he had passed the second slope on his back!

"*Sacré Bompard!*" said Bézuquet; "he came back to us with his story all the same!" Then they all laughed, and rubbed their hands, while outside, the band, which they in vain attempted to silence, furiously attacked the Funeral March of Tartarin of Tarascon.

"*Vé* Costecalde, how yellow he is!" murmured Pascalon to Bravida, indicating the armourer, who had risen to cede his chair to the old President, whose good face shone brightly. Bravida, always sententious, replied in a whisper, as he perceived Costecalde superseded—relegated to the rank of subaltern: "The luck of the Abbé Mandaire; from parish priest he was relegated to curate."[1]

And then the meeting resumed.

---

[1] "La fortune de l'abbé Mandaire—
De curé il devint vicaire!"—H F.

Table of Contents

I

An apparition on the Rigi-Kulm.—Who is he?—What was said at the *table d'hôte*.—Rice and Prunes.—An improvised ball.—The Unknown signs his name in the hotel register.—P. C. A.   **Page 1**

II

Tarascon, five minutes' stoppage.—The Alpine Club.—Explanation of P. C. A.—Rabbits of the warren and of the cabbage-garden.—"This is my will."—The *Sirop de Cadavre*.—First ascent.—Tartarin mounts his spectacles . . .   29

Table of Contents

III

An alarm on the Rigi.—Be cool! be cool!—The Alpine horn.—What Tartarin found on his looking glass when he awoke.—Perplexity.—He asks for a guide by telephone 65

IV

On board the steamer.—Rain.—The hero of Tarascon salutes the Shades.—The truth about William Tell.—Disillusion—Tartarin of Tarascon never existed!—" Té! Bompard!" . . 88

V

Confidences in a tunnel 117

VI

The Pass of the Brünig.—Tartarin falls into the hands of the Nihilists.—Disappearance of an Italian tenor and an Avignon rope.—New exploits of a *chasseur de casquettes.*—Pan! Pan! 120

VII

Night at Tarascon.—Where is he?—Anxiety.—The *cigales du Cours* demand Tartarin.—Martyrdom of a Tarascon saint.—The Alpine Club.—What happened at the chemist's.—Help! Bézuquet. 161

VIII

Memorable dialogue between the Jungfrau and Tartarin.—A Nihilist *salon*.—The duel with hunting-knives.—Horrible nightmare.—" 'Tis I whom you seek, gentlemen!"—Strange reception of the Tarascon delegates at the Hôtel Meyer 185

IX

At the sign of "The Faithful Chamois" 213

X

The ascent of the Jungfrau.—*Vé!* the oxen!—The Kennedy *crampons* do not answer; neither does the lamp.—Appearance of masked men at the chalet.—The President in the *crevasse*.—He leaves his spectacles behind him.—On the peaks.—Tartarin a deity 233

XI

En route for Tarascon!—The Lake of Geneva.—Tartarin suggests a visit to Bonnivard's cell.—A short dialogue amid the roses.—All the band under lock and key.—The unfortunate Bonnivard.—A certain rope made in Avignon comes to light 261

Table of Contents

XII

The Hôtel Baltet at Chamonix.—That smell of garlic!—Concerning the uses of the cord in Alpine excursions.—Shake hands!—A pupil of Schopenhauer's.—At the Grands-Mulets.—"Tartarin, I must speak to you."   293

XIII

The Catastrophe 325

XIV

Epilogue .   . . 349

www.ingramcontent.com/pod-product-compliance
Lightning Source LLC
Chambersburg PA
CBHW021622250426
43672CB00037B/344